266.1

9L.

WORLD LIBRARY OF SACRED MUSIC
1846 WESTWOOD AVE.
CINCINNATI 14, OHIO

THE MISSION OF
THE CHURCH

The Mission of
the Church

CHARLES COUTURIER, S.J.

*

TRANSLATED FROM THE FRENCH
BY A. V. LITTLEDALE

HELICON PRESS
BALTIMORE

HELICON PRESS
5305 EAST DRIVE, BALTIMORE 27, MD

*First published in France under the title
'Mission de l'Église' by Éditions de l'Orante,
Paris 1957
This English edition first published 1960*

LIBRARY OF CONGRESS CATALOG CARD NO: 59·9914

PRINTED IN GREAT BRITAIN BY NORTHUMBERLAND PRESS
LTD., GATESHEAD ON TYNE. NIHIL OBSTAT HUBERTUS
RICHARDS, S.T.L., L.S.S., CENSOR DEPUTATUS. IM-
PRIMATUR E. MORROGH BERNARD, VIC. GEN. WEST-
MONASTERII, DIE 26A JANUARII, 1959

CONTENTS

ACKNOWLEDGMENTS

We are indebted to His Eminence the Cardinal, Archbishop of Westminster and Messrs. Burns Oates & Washbourne Ltd. for extracts from the late Monsignor R. A. Knox's translation of the Bible; Messrs. Sheed & Ward Ltd. and Sheed & Ward Inc. New York for extracts from *Religion and Culture* by Jacques Maritain, published in America in *Essays in Order* ed. by Christopher Dawson & T. F. Burns, copyright 1939 Sheed & Ward Inc.

INTRODUCTION TO
THE ENGLISH TRANSLATION

BY THE VERY REV. M. J. WALSH, S.M.A.

WITH the rapid missionary expansion of the
Church and the increasing number of Ency-
clicals and Papal pronouncements regarding
the spread of the Gospel in pagan lands, every new work
dealing with missionary theology is a welcome addition,
but more particularly one in English. The dearth of
material on this subject in the English language, out of
all proportion to the number of English-speaking
missionaries, presents a curious anomaly, and makes
this translation of Charles Couturier's *Mission de
l'Église* a book that will supply a long-felt need.

In his Introduction, the writer acknowledges a debt
of gratitude to Father de Menasce, O.P., without the aid
of whose valuable manuscript notes, constant criticism,
authoritative advice and, above all, inspiration, the book
would never have been written. At the 1955 Conference
of Ecclesiastical Studies held in England, I had the
pleasure of meeting Father de Menasce, who came from
Paris to read one of the papers. Even our informal
discussions on missionary work revealed his extensive
knowledge of the cultural and social problems affecting
the evangelization of new territories, and his deep con-

cern about the chaos which a clash of cultures could bring about unless they were harmoniously fused. I knew at once that here was a book worth studying, and I was not disappointed.

Charles Couturier explains that in spite of the constant stream of works devoted to missionary theology, many possessing considerable merit, most suffer from being restricted to a part of the mission field, and appear as isolated monographs. The comparatively few textbooks which aim at co-ordinating the various materials are generally too analytical in treatment to give an overall picture of the principles governing missionary activity. The special merit of this book is that it attempts to supply a comprehensive view of the Church's missionary function.

The author does not offer an exhaustive or text-book treatment, but his very readable presentation adequately outlines the problems confronting modern missionary endeavour. He takes full account of the fact that peoples are no longer culturally static, but the influence of Western Society and of the Church itself is inevitably playing an important role in shaping the destiny of new countries, and effecting, as a consequence, consciously or unconsciously, a religious, social, educational and political ferment. All this, and the rising tide of national aspirations, makes the task of the present-day missionary more delicate than that of his predecessors.

The mission of the Church is to preach the Gospel to every creature, to establish the Kingdom of God where it has not yet penetrated or where it has not been fully developed, and to make divine life accessible to new peoples by translating the message of the eternal Word into their language and culture. The Church, in its efforts to accomplish this, is viewed by the writer, through the eyes of the Gospel, as the great Tree sprung from a grain of mustard seed. The missionary is visualized as the gardener whose task it is not only to graft on new main branches, but to ensure that the graft takes properly and that good fruit is produced. This grafting process may be called adaptation. While Christ is the Master Gardener and the fruit ultimately depends on the flow of sanctifying grace, it has been left to the Hierarchical organization of the Church to specify the precise means of establishing contact with peoples, to watch over this grafting process so that they may better understand Christ's message and the Christian way of life.

The Church itself, we know, was not an entirely new creation, and the principles of adaptation have always governed its missionary activity. We read in the Gospels how understandingly Christ accommodated His heavenly doctrine to the mental capacity of His hearers. The early Church, which had taken root in Palestine, did not hesitate to enrich its tradition by drawing on the cultures of many peoples. Ecclesiastical law bears the imprint of the Roman Empire, theologians borrowed from Greek philosophy, and Christian artists found inspiration in their pagan environment. Usages connected with the cult of local deities were purified, and while the material elements remained the same, the prayers which consecrated them to idols were eliminated and replaced by invocations in the name of God and His saints.

During the post-Renaissance period—especially during the age of discovery—a change of approach to the evangelization of pagan peoples could be discerned. For a variety of reasons, political, economic or sometimes from lack of knowledge, it generally became the fashion to suppose that all non-Western culture was crude and barbarous and had to be uprooted. This misplaced zeal for their own culture caused colonizers and missionaries to forget that the human qualities of people are the gift of God Himself, that knowledge of the moral law was not the sole prerogative of Christians, but was imprinted on the fleshy tablets of every man's heart. Yet in spite of an Instruction of the Sacred Congregation of Propaganda in the seventeenth century, which urged missionaries not to reject or impair the usages of new peoples except in so far as they were corrupt, but rather to preserve and protect them, in spite of the example and pleadings of such apostolic men as Father de Nobili in India and Matteo Ricci in China, the practice of imposing the supposedly superior pattern of their own Western culture on conquered peoples was continued.

The difficulties of those early missionaries, however, must be appreciated. In the face of so much 'fetish' worship, it was not easy to realize that beneath the cult of shapeless divinities which thirsted for blood, even human blood, beneath the seeming jumbled mass of distortion and contradiction, beneath the ritual dances and even the orgies, lay a chain of doctrine and often a complex religious system. It is often ignorance rather than perversion which is responsible for the errors in pagan moral judgments, for without the aid of supernatural light, the notion of right and wrong may become clouded by custom, concupiscence or expediency. Our predecessors in the field, it should be remembered, had not the benefit of ethnographic or missiological studies which have helped to make intelligible for us many conflicting beliefs and customs, and have opened the door to a greater appreciation of the intrinsic and spiritual values of indigenous cultural traditions.

No one would deny the importance of a sympathetic approach to existing pagan cultures where the whole religious and social background of the people to be contacted is different from that of the missionaries. Nevertheless, the bearer of God's message should not fall into the error of some anthropologists and try to explain all difficulties in terms of culture contact. It is true, as Charles Couturier states it, that inhuman social conditions and the struggle against injustice and destitution can hinder access to the Christian life, and the missionary must be actively concerned with setting right elements of native culture which are at variance with the moral law. Yet we cannot conclude that success in preaching the Gospel will come only after the cultural and social evils have been put right. Humanization does not necessarily precede evangelization.

The missionary must also guard against the other extreme in thinking that the Church, allied to a particu-

lar culture in so far as it lives and expresses it, makes
no impression because of its Western garb. He may
feel that the Church should be restored to its primitive
universality, which in effect would mean taking on a
new and individual culture—that is, humanizing the
Church before evangelizing the people. But the Church,
as Charles Couturier points out, is not a purely human
institution, and its contact with people is more than a
meeting of cultures. Grace can be communicated, and
the word of God heard, as we know from the Gospel
and the history of the early Church, before cultural
differences have been smoothed over. Since Christian
morality is illuminated by Revelation and completely
penetrated by grace, and grace takes hold of every facet
of human life, the Church by its temporal action aims
not only at creating conditions useful or indispensable
to its supernatural action, but also at impregnating the
temporal sphere with a specifically Christian spirit.

Charles Couturier presents the Church as a living
organism possessing a dynamic equilibrium which makes
it capable of change provided its essential structure is
preserved. In so far as the Church, without ceasing to
be Divine, is a human society, its actual way of life
reflects man's way of thinking. All tradition is not
dogma, every custom is not sacrosanct, even if both the
one and the other are orthodox and beneficial. There is
room for adaptation, in which he outlines three main
elements: Divine Revelation, the objective content of
Christian dogma which is universal in its application
and admits of no modification; at the opposite ends to

this is the human cultural expression of that objective reality which is changeable and multiform and refers to extra-liturgical feasts, sacred art, family customs, etc.; in between these two, the writer places ecclesiastical tradition which intimately binds the human elements to the Divine. It does not exclude all variety, and its unity is compatible with plurality of forms, as in varying liturgies, the new Paschal Vigil, etc. It is clear, therefore, as Father Voss states it, that while the essence of Christianity which is of Divine origin can admit of no accommodation, yet, under Divine Providence, the human and consequently accidental development is not of metaphysical or universal value but admits of change and modification.

This compact volume, so richly interspersed with references from Scripture and examples from the history of the Church, presenting in concentrated form the principles, methods, merits and dangers of adaptation and its concrete application to the liturgy of the Church, family and social customs and political institutions, will be welcomed, I feel, not only by missionaries whose specific task is to preach the Faith among non-Christian peoples, but by all; for the spread of the Gospel is the duty of everyone who has the interest of Christ at heart.

The book may well be described as an extended paraphrase of the words of the late Pope Pius XII in *Summi Pontificatus*, where he says that the Church, the faithful depository of the teaching of Divine wisdom, cannot and does not think of depreciating or disdaining the particular characteristics which each people, with jealous and intelligible pride, cherish and retain as a precious heritage. Her aim is a supernatural union in all-embracing love, deeply felt and practised, and not the unity which is external and superficial and, by that very fact, weak.

The Pope reminds us that the Church has shown in her missionary enterprises that such a principle of action is the guiding star of her universal apostolate. Pioneer research and investigation, involving sacrifice, devotedness and love on the part of her missionaries, have been undertaken in order to facilitate a more deeply appreciative insight into the most varied civilizations and to put their spiritual values to account for a living and vital preaching of the Gospel of Christ. 'The Church has never disdained the doctrines held by pagans, but instead, after freeing them from all admixture of error, has completed and perfected them by the work of Christian wisdom.' All those who enter the Church, whatever be their origin or their speech, must know that they have equal rights as children in the house of the Lord, where the law of Christ and the peace of Christ prevail.

PREFACE

For many years, there has been a constant stream of works devoted to missionary theology and, in particular, missionary action, and many of them have considerable merit. Most, however, have the drawback of being restricted to a part of the field, and appear as monographs on isolated subjects. The few text-books which aim at co-ordinating the various materials are too analytical in treatment to give a comprehensive view of the Church's missionary function.

I have been tempted to supply this comprehensive view, and may be judged, by the result, to have been over-ambitious. However that may be, I would point out that this book lays no claim to be a treatise on missiology. As matters stand at present, both the object and bounds of that science have yet to be fixed; and, in any case, some questions, in my view essential, are only touched upon here.

My aim is the modest one of clarifying the theological principles and sociological laws which combine to govern missionary action, of tracing the elaborate linkage of its different facets, and of setting each problem in the context of the whole life of the Church. The simplified treatment needs expansion in a great variety of directions. It is purposely brief so that the reader may embrace the missionary Church in a single view, and learn to see the detailed problems in their true light.

I must not fail to acknowledge my debt to Father de Menasce, O.P. This work would never have been written if he had not inspired it, if he had not shown me his valuable manuscript notes, and aided me by his constant criticism and authoritative advice. Whatever value it may have it owes to him.

INTRODUCTION

'Y o u, therefore, must go out, making disciples of all nations' (Mt. 28: 19). There was a time when the Church might have believed she had fulfilled this injunction, but the sixteenth-century explorers of America, Africa and Asia opened out an immense field of action whose existence was hitherto scarcely suspected. The Church suddenly became aware that it comprised only a minority of the human race, and set itself vigorously to spread the Gospel throughout the new continents. Its success did not match its early expectations. All races, indeed, had their Christian members, but their number still remains slight in relation to the masses of the unconverted.

Consequently, doubt arose as to the whole manner of approach, and as to whether the methods used should not be revised. On reflection, it became more and more evident, particularly in the last half-century, that this could not be resolved independently of the wider problem of the true end of missionary action, of the precise need it was meant to fill. This, it was said, was 'to make Christians where there had been only pagans'— a formula which certainly conveyed the Church's mind from its beginning, but yet left some uncertainty.

To be 'Christian' means to acknowledge Christ to be the incarnate Son of God, the one Saviour of the human race; it means receiving the light of his message, accepting the seal of his Baptism, and being thereby incorporated into his Church, in order to receive the communication of his life.

Destined, as it is, to continue the work of its Head, the Church is modelled on him. By its mystical union with Christ, it bears in itself his divine life, and conveys it through the sacraments committed to the hierarchy. Thus it is at once invisible and visible; under these two aspects, which cannot be dissociated, it is essentially a mystery of the supernatural order.

Through its members, and the mission entrusted to them of proclaiming Christ and bringing men to live by him, the Church comes to be linked with cultures that are the outward expression of the life of all kinds of peoples. For it has to translate the eternal Word into their tongues to make it accessible to them, and to intervene, more or less directly, in the social, economic and political problems of the world to illuminate them by the light of eternity. In that way, though not 'of the world', it is a social entity, one entirely orientated to its supernatural end.

These two functions—expression of the Word and social action—though bound up with the supernatural work of the Church, are not to be confused with it; they are only particular conditions of its performance, and are due to the fact that the Church, while living essentially by the very life of Christ, acts on men by men who are its rulers and members.

Consequently, what characterizes the Christian as

such is his participation in the life of Christ. This is not just a superstructure added to his natural life without changing it in any way; but, penetrating it while remaining distinct, it works in it a transformation which enables him to live his whole life on the supernatural level. The Christian is, none the less, liable to shortcomings, either through failure to direct a part of his actions towards God, or through wilful sin. Though, in itself, his spiritual ascent depends essentially on the grace given to him and his reception of it, it depends too, in a certain way, on the actual environment of his life. The Christian is, after all, a human being, and, as such, subject to the social influences that bear on him. Apart from special grace, his ascent will be facilitated or hindered according as the Christians around him more or less faithfully express the divine message, show its effect on the most concrete details of life, and draw him, by their example, to take up a fully Christian attitude.

Are we, by contrast, to consider as a 'pagan' anyone whose life is not enlightened by Christ? It is tempting to apply the term in this way, yet, despite its elasticity, it is inappropriate. Jews and Moslems know and adore the true God, and accept his Revelation; what they lack is its fulness, and so they are commonly called by Christians 'infidels'. Over against them are the 'atheists', who reject God absolutely; but it may be that those who claim this title reject only a vain idol, since, in fact, their idea of God is false and inadmissible; in their fidelity to the Good as they see it, they render secret homage to the true God. Between these extremes lies a vast field where numerous religions, varying in purity, arouse in their adherents some sense of adoration and prayer, of justice and charity, but in an obscure manner, gropingly, and with an admixture of error.

The spiritual values accessible to the non-Christian vary according to the particular cultural group of which he forms a part and according to his own personal dispositions. It is impossible to tell how far he is capable of advancing in the knowledge and love of God by means of symbols that are inherently defective, hiding from him the light while, at the same time, allowing it to filter through. He is, like the Christian, one of the 'redeemed'; the blood of Christ flowed for him, and merited for him forgiveness and grace. Even though he does not acknowledge Christ as his Lord and God, because the means for doing so have not been given him, he is not thereby deprived of the graces necessary for his salvation. He is offered them, and, if his response is generous, he lives already with a genuinely super-natural life.

The division between Christians and non-Christians is thus seen to be far less profound than is commonly imagined, since both the one and the other may share in the divine life, and are capable of losing it. It might even appear that this life is offered to all men by the mediation of Christ alone, without the Church having to play any active part other than making known the source to those unaware of it, and gathering together those who do know. In that case, the preaching of

Christ by the Church would no longer be urgently
necessary, and would seem to be dangerous rather than
useful; for there is no doubt that it disquiets the conscience of many who have lived long in ignorance of
Christ. There are men of good will—we confine ourselves to them—who have striven to be faithful to their
interior lights, and, at the same time, to their inherited
religious traditions, when a missionary arrives to tell
them they have been living in darkness and error.
From their point of view, he is a foreigner coming to
cast doubt on the ancestral wisdom and, still more, on
the spiritual way they have been following. It may be
that, confident in their own experience, they close their
minds to his message. Or else it may happen that they
acknowledge the justice of his criticism of their religion.
In this case, the unsettlement of their minds could lead
them in very different directions: it could open them to
Christ, or shut them up in agnosticism or even atheism.
If the religion by which they thought themselves to live
were open to doubt, could not the same be said of all
the others? An access of light does not facilitate salvation so much as increase responsibility, for God, who is
just, judges men according to the gifts they have
received. Consequently, the conclusion is sometimes
drawn that it is better to leave men in good faith than,
by preaching the Gospel, to cause them serious
disturbance.

But that would show a failure to understand why
Christ founded the Church and commanded the
apostles to evangelize and baptize the nations. It would

be to misunderstand, too, the Incarnation of the Word and his Redemption, 'to the Jews a discouragement, to the Gentiles mere folly' (1 Cor. 1: 23); and to lose the sense of the mystery of salvation.

By an absolutely unmerited gift of the love of God, man is called to enter, by participation, the very life of the Blessed Trinity, a destiny beyond his natural reach; moreover, he has turned away from it by sin, and is unable to take a single step towards its fulfilment unless God takes the initiative. To save himself means to accept the gift of God and surrender to his love. It is not for him to impose a measure on the gifts of God; he must accept them or perish. The danger is great, for the divine love makes formidable demands, but it is, too, the precious pearl of great price whose possession alone can fill the needs of man (Mt. 13: 45-46).

The missionary activity of the Church is to be understood only in the light of God's plan for the human race. Once this is made clear, it will be possible to determine the laws of its origin and growth, and to see the obstacles it has to surmount.

I

THE DIVINE PLAN OF SALVATION

I N the sphere of salvation, the initiative comes entirely from God, and so we have to find out what he expects of us; no one is entitled to assume the power of directing our destiny, unless he has received it from God. But how could we direct our course unaided? God, had he judged it good, could doubtless have confined himself to speaking to each in the depths of the heart; in fact, he chose a way more conformable to the nature with which he had endowed man: 'In old days, God spoke to our fathers in many ways and by many means, through the prophets; now at last in these times he has spoken to us with a Son to speak for him; a Son, whom he has appointed to inherit all things' (Heb. 1: 1-2). That is the salient fact in the history of mankind, the primary Mission of which all others are either the preparation or the fulfilment.

Mission of the Divine Persons

God made himself one of us; that was the means of salvation devised by the love of the Trinity. Through the Incarnation, the divine Light itself shines in the world (Jn. 1: 5). Consequently, the revelation given was bound to be definitive and complete; it comprises all truth and admits no error. It is not just a theory brought by Christ to the world, alongside so many others. The Good Tidings with which he was entrusted are that 'God so loved the world that he gave up his only-begotten Son, so that those who believe in him may not perish, but may have eternal life' (Jn. 3: 16). He is himself our salvation; for he is the Way every man has to travel to ascend to God, the Truth which enlightens the world, the Life which triumphs over death and draws mankind after him in his resurrection.

As 'missionary of God', he claims nothing for himself, but, in everything, conforms to the intentions of the Father: 'The learning which I impart is not my own, it comes from him who sent me' (Jn. 7: 16); 'The Son cannot do anything at his own pleasure, he can only do what he sees his Father doing; what the Father does is what the Son does in his turn' (Jn. 5: 19); 'My meat is to do the will of him who sent me, and to accomplish the task he gave me' (Jn. 4: 34). In return, the Father bears him witness (Jn. 6: 44-45; 8: 18), and gives him all power on heaven and earth. The salvation of men depends on the attitude they take up in regard to him: 'He who believes in the Son possesses eternal life, whereas he who refuses to believe in the Son will never see life; God's displeasure hangs over him continually' (Jn. 3: 36).

As the 'one mediator' (1 Tim. 2: 5), Christ alone possesses the power to make us 'children of God' (Jn. 1: 12). The sole Saviour, he offers himself as a sacrifice for all men, so redeeming them from sin, and gaining for them access to God. No one can add anything to the perfection of his work; but, to gain its fruits, man has himself to take on freely the entire offering made in his name by Christ. 'To bring together into one all God's children, scattered far and wide' (Jn. 11: 52), the Incarnate Word, in his turn, sent out missionaries, the Spirit and the Church.

The Spirit 'will bear witness' to Christ (Jn. 15: 26). He does not speak of himself, and has no other message than that of Christ (Jn. 16: 13). But the divine Word had come up against carnal minds, where it was almost doomed to sterility; the Spirit penetrates within them to open them out and make the Word fertile. With unexampled force, he breaks in upon the world to spread abroad the Church planted by Christ (Acts 9: 13), and to form it into the perfect body of Christ. His essential mission is to penetrate it with charity, that is, to make it participate in the movement of love by which the divine Persons give themselves to each other in a perfect gift. So the Church is made capable of responding duly to the full gift which Christ made to it of himself; it is drawn in to the life of the Trinity.

The Mission of the Church

The Church brings the effective antidote to sin, and to the disunity which is its consequence. Adam's sin set man in opposition to God, but bore fruit, too, in the murder of Abel, and issued in the mystery of the tower of Babel, which is the mystery of the divisions among men. The divine action, on the other hand, is essentially unifying. The Incarnation and Redemption destroyed the chasm sin caused between God and man, and received their fulfilment in the mystery of Pentecost.

Humanity, of its very nature, has a tendency to realize its unity in fact; but it is impeded by the seeds of division sowed by sin. The Word came down on earth to destroy these seeds, and to offer men a unity undreamt of, a participation in the divine Unity itself: 'It is not only for them [the apostles] that I pray; I pray for those who are to find faith in me through their word; that they may all be one; that they too may be one in us, as thou, Father, art in me, and I in thee; so that the world may come to believe that it is thou who hast sent me' (Jn. 17: 20-21).

In becoming incarnate, the Word took a human nature and raised it up to his divine personality; the unity thus realized in Christ is perfect, immediate, and absolute. By the very intensity of its action on that human nature, it influences mankind in general, and forms it into the mystical body of Christ, the Church. This is a social organism of the supernatural order, which, without destroying the personality of its individual members, effects an inner transformation of their life. It does not take to itself a nature at a particular moment of time, but gathers in, through the succeeding generations, all varieties of individuals, groups and peoples; it is therefore bound up with temporal conditions, and those of generation and growth. The union of Christ with men, of which it is the realization, is the remote image of that between the human and divine natures in the person of Christ; it is no less real, and infinitely deeper, than that of any purely human society.

The Church is the new People, heir of the promises to Israel. It is the Vine wherein circulates the divine life; a branch cut off from it is only good to be cast into the fire. It is the Body of which Christ is the source of unity and the Head; the Temple where he has set up his dwelling, and of which he is the corner-stone. It is the Spouse he has redeemed and purified, to whom he is bound with an enduring love, and which he brings to reign with him in his glory. It is his Presence continued in the world, and extended to every part of space and time.

Consequently, it is entrusted with carrying on his mission: 'I came upon an errand from my Father, and now I am sending you out in my turn' (Jn. 20: 21). 'You therefore must go out, making disciples of all nations, and baptizing them in the name of the Father, and of the Son, and of the Holy Ghost, teaching them to observe all the commandments which I have given you. And behold I am with you all through the days that are coming until the consummation of the world' (Mt. 28: 19-20). It is so identified with Christ that men pass judgment on themselves by the reception they give it: 'He who listens to you, listens to me; he who despises you, despises me; and he who despises me, despises him that sent me' (Lk. 10: 16; cf. Jn. 13: 20).

The Church is a necessary means to salvation, for it

'exists for nothing else than to make all men sharers in the graces of salvation brought by the Redemption, by spreading the reign of Christ through the entire world' (Pius XI, *Rerum Ecclesiae*); but it is itself salvation, in so far as it carries into effect the union of men with Christ. It would be wrong to oppose a Church in this world, visible and hierarchical, to a heavenly Church, invisible and mystical. Although these two aspects of the Church do not completely coincide, yet they are not to be considered apart. For, on the one hand, the hierarchical Church brings about, by functions partly visible, but still 'mysterious'—sacramental and juridical—a mystical unity whose range, moreover, extends beyond its visible frontiers; and, on the other, since its members are men, it is involved in earthly affairs which are not its proper work, and are always subordinate to its supernatural functions. For that reason, the hierarchical Church alone is the recipient of the promises, and embodies the presence of Christ on earth to draw men into the life of Heaven. It is one and the same City of God that is built upon earth and has its foundation in Heaven; it is the same Body of Christ that grows by degrees and purifies its members here, and that is already triumphant in Heaven. 'Anyone looking on the Church,' affirms St Gregory of Nyssa, 'truly looks on Christ.'

It follows that drawing near to God, confessing Christ, entering the Church, are one and the same thing. Doubtless a man may live by grace, without having any visible relation with the Church, when he has not yet had the opportunity to recognize it for what it is. Yet he already belongs to it in a hidden manner; without being aware of it, he is nourished by its sap; he participates secretly in the fulness of life and light it alone can communicate. When the Church is shown to him, it only remains for him to ratify, by asking for Baptism, what was already the meaning of his life; if he does not do so, he turns away from God and is false to himself. All grace is from Christ, and no one can be saved without belonging to the Church.

Here we see the fearful responsibility of the heads and members of the Church on earth. Their persistence in claiming to be the sole depositories of the mystery of salvation seems to be pride, and is a cause of scandal. None the less, it is but humble fidelity to the mission received from God, humble certitude that, in spite of their personal unworthiness, they are the ambassadors of the Church of Christ, which, possessed of the message of salvation, cannot keep it selfishly for its own benefit, but must proclaim it throughout the earth. As guardian of the sources of life flowing from the opened side of Christ, which are alone capable of quenching the thirst of man, it has to use them to fecundate the whole universe. From the very beginning of the human race, men, despite all their faults, have been groping and straining in the search for God, who calls them in their inmost being. The Church cannot be indifferent to their strivings, when it has the secret to bring them to fulfilment.

'The Missions'

It is one and the same work to make men live by the life of Christ and so bring them salvation, and to strive for the growth of the Church till it reaches its full stature; it will not be accomplished till the end of time. Therein consists the essential mission of the Church, and this involves different tasks.

In its beginning, there was a *foundation* period, inaugurated by Christ, and entrusted by him to the apostles assisted by the Holy Ghost. Thus the Church was already endowed with all its essential organs; it was brought into the world and no power could drive it out.

Next, there had to be continuous advance of the reign of God among the peoples where the Church had grown to the extent that its riches were actually available to every person of good will. This was its *pastoral activity*.

At the same time, it had to set up the kingdom of God in places where it had not yet penetrated, or where it was not fully developed. This is the traditional meaning of its 'missionary activity', and the proper sense of that expression.

This activity is, of its nature, transitory, and issues in pastoral action. It is not a question of founding the *Church*—this has been done once and for all—but of bringing to birth *new local Churches*,[1] that is to say,

[1] St Paul uses the word 'Church' for the Christian community in a particular town (the Church of Antioch, Corinth, etc.). Very soon, it acquired the meaning of the universal Church, the mystical

bringing the divine life to new peoples. It is a question of grafting[1] new main branches on the great tree sprung from the grain of mustard seed (Mt. 13: 31), and of taking care that the graft takes properly and bears lasting fruit. The new local Churches must be assured in their growth till they are visible and stable enough to ensure that the faith is effectively promulgated throughout their country.

Consequently, the Church has the duty to establish itself, not only where it has never been before, that is among non-Christian peoples, but also where it exists in an incomplete state, as among heretical and schismatic Christians. It might be the case that a part, or a particular level, of the population of a Christian country is a closed group without any real contact with the Church; such a group would be the subject of the Church's missionary action in the strict sense.

The Church, once founded, has a double work,

body of Christ. Both these meanings remain traditional in the Christian vocabulary; but they could give rise to misunderstanding. It is important to observe that the *direct* object of missionary action is to set up a *community* of believers where there was none before, and *thereby* to co-operate in the mysterious growth of the Body of Christ.

[1] The symbol of grafting is a classical one from the time of St Paul (Rom. 11: 16-24). Normally, cultivated plants are grafted on to wild trees and feed on their sap; but the graft succeeds only in so far as the former is enabled to produce its characteristic fruit. This is the feature St Paul stresses, but reversing the normal relationship, led on, no doubt, by the symbol of the vine (Jn. 15:1-6). For Christ is the one source of life to all men, and the Church brings this life to them, and changes them into 'God's people'. We consider, at the end of the book, the contribution the various peoples bring to the Church.

pastoral and missionary; and therefore it might be thought that the latter is the province exclusively of a section of the Church devoted especially to the purpose. This would be a dangerous error, impairing the Church in its essential nature. Missionary action belongs to the whole body of the Church, for it derives directly from its nature and is the expression of it.

Primarily, missionary action devolves on the hierarchy, taken as a body, as heir of the apostles, for it is the possession of the priesthood in its fulness that confers the right and imposes the duty to proclaim Christ and communicate his life to men. The other members, priests and laity, share in it, but not in the same manner and degree. No one can renounce his part, for the very life of the Church is involved, and each Christian, inasmuch as he benefits from this, has his share of responsibility for it.

All contribute to the work by their union with Christ and by the spiritual riches they gain for the Church. In addition, some are called to discharge such primary functions as preaching and baptizing. Others perform subsidiary tasks, such as preparing souls for the acceptance of Christ, or restoring those natural foundations necessary for the Church to build on. Still others are engaged in the training of missionaries, or support the missions by their active interest and contributions. The vocations are various, but all are necessary, and each person has the duty to respond to God's particular call.

It is through this variety that the Church is enabled to discharge the complex functions implied in missionary activity. Now that we have perceived the general end and necessity of this kind of activity, we must attempt to set out its main features.[1] It is centred always on the proclamation of the faith and the imparting of the divine life; but since it is concerned, too, with forming communities living the Christian life, it has to include a number of accessory functions, all bearing, more or less closely, on the life of the Church.

[1] We have in view, essentially, the mission to non-Christian countries. The same guiding principles apply in other cases, but with important modifications.

2

BEGINNINGS OF A CHURCH

'NOBODY,' says Christ, 'can come to me without being attracted towards me by the father who sent me' (Jn. 6: 44). It is from their inner selves above all, on the call of the Father, under the hidden influence of the merits of Christ placed at the disposition of the Church, by the action of the Holy Ghost by whom 'the love of God has been poured out in our hearts' (Rom. 5: 5), that men come to seek light and life in the Church of Christ.

The missionary is sent by the Church to announce the Good Tidings that God loves man, and to invite men to give glory to the Most High and to draw living water from its one source (Jn. 4: 10-14; 7: 37); and he is not to expect that his efforts to dispose men to understand and live the divine word should produce conversions as an effect following its cause. Faith does not result, properly speaking, from his influence, any more than from a purely human decision of his hearers; it is above all a grace of God offered to man.

Hence, there is no need for surprise if it pleases God to show himself to men and bring them to his Church, without making them go through the normal stages of preparation. He was pleased to grant Cornelius the centurion exceptional graces, and to sanctify him by sending the Holy Ghost, even before he had received Baptism; it was, moreover, a sign for the Church that being a gentile was no hindrance to becoming a cate-chumen (Acts 10-11). God intervened in just as sovereign a fashion in the life of St Paul and that of many others. It pleases him, too, to draw men, in a more hidden manner, by all kinds of antecedent graces, arousing in them, or in some at least, a desire for the good, a thirst for purity of life. The missionary must understand that the ways of God transcend the ordinary, and must respect 'the divine moment' in souls.

This need not make him undervalue the necessity of the task entrusted to him. His action is an instrumental one; it is to bring home the nature and urgency of the divine call, and to help each person to respond to it. For this purpose, the missionary must present the mess-age of Christ in a language all can understand, strive to remove the prejudices in the minds of his hearers, make them feel the attractiveness of the life of which he is the bearer, and teach them to make it their own. These are all aspects, inseparable from one another, of his sole function, which is to form sons of God.

Seen from the outside, his apostolate might seem like some form or other of 'propaganda'. Originally, this term signified the Church's action in spreading the faith. In the most usual sense of the word to-day, a pejorative one, it implies a deceptive or perverse kind of activity; 'propaganda', as now understood, is concerned with neither the good of men nor truth, but skilfully flatters human passion, and seduces the imagination in order to gain command of the mind, and reduce it, by a course of oppression, to a state in which it is no longer free in its judgments.

The missionary also makes use of human means: the spoken word, the Press, the radio, and the rest; but these serve his purpose only if employed in an entirely different spirit. It is impossible for force or pressure of any kind to cause that free homage of man to God that missionary action aims to produce. Just as Christ triumphed over Satan in the desert (Mt. 4: 1-11), the missionary has to resist any temptation to lose sight of the true supernatural character of his work, its means as well as its end. Great holiness is needed to handle worldly instruments without being dominated by them. While respectful of the liberty of men, the missionary must yet make it plain that he has something of the greatest value to offer them; he must do so peacefully and disinterestedly, if he wishes the divine word to make itself heard.

His primary function is to proclaim Christ, and to this all the rest of his work is subordinate. Planting the Church is not, in the first place, erecting buildings, nor is it creating a local clergy, nor even establishing Catholic worship; it is announcing that 'the kingdom of heaven is at hand'; 'the kingdom of God is here, within you' (Mt. 3: 2; Lk. 17: 21).

How the Church is presented

At first the missionary, to gain a hearing for the divine word, will be drawn to express in other languages, however roughly, the familiar terms of his religion, and to suggest to his hearers the adoption of practices integral to his own life as a Christian. It will not be long before he realizes the difficulties confronting him. They arise principally from the fact that the Church has developed notably in the course of centuries, and that, in addition, the people to be evangelized have a whole background of religious history of their own.

The divine seed of the Church was cast originally on the soil of Palestine, and soon spread over the shores of the Mediterranean. Christ himself fixed, in sovereign and permanent fashion, its essential features: a message to deliver, sacramental acts to be performed, powers of order and jurisdiction entrusted to Peter and the apostolic college, together with their successors. But the rulers of the Church, in the course of succeeding ages, were to define the means of making contact with men, of enabling them to reach a better understanding of the message of Christ, and of training them to lead a fully Christian life.

For this purpose, the Church was led to work out a theology setting before the mind the inexhaustible mystery of God, to develop a spirituality which teaches how to live thereby, to envelop the sacramental acts in a setting of gestures and prayers for their more fruitful working, to create a parochial organization for closer contact with the people, and to define their duties in a code of law.

The Church, since it was obliged to see that the Christian spirit should inform its members in every detail of their lives, could not fail to take account of their problems of everyday life. It was led, in consequence, to approve certain devotions and forbid others, to pass judgment on books, even secular ones, and also on artistic matters, and to define, on many points, how the Christian ought to conduct his social relationships.

This work, so wide in scope, fell to the pastors of the Church in the first instance, but also for various reasons to all its members. While it gave rise to original creations, it was accomplished, in large measure, by drawing on the cultures of the peoples where the Church took root and grew. Ecclesiastical administration and law bear a clear imprint of the Roman Empire. Theologians made use of Greek philosophy, thought out afresh, as a valuable means for the understanding of the Christian mysteries. Christian artists drew freely on native tradition for their inspiration. Liturgical vestments were originally garments in ordinary use. All kinds of customs which formerly referred to the divinities of rivers, harvests, fecundity, and others, were purified and sanctified; the places or the seasons with which they were associated, the material elements used for the purpose, could be retained, but the prayers offered to idols were eliminated, and replaced by a blessing in the name of God, and by the invocation of saints.

This is how elements of a culture were adopted by the Church in the course of its history. Some of them, taken over into liturgy, theology, law, affect its life deeply and intimately; many others have only a superficial influence.

The Church has become a great tree from which new main branches must be made to grow. The work involved may not be any more arduous than it was in the Church's infancy, but it is particularly delicate. The essential features of the Church have not changed, but they are more sharply outlined, more completely expressed. Their mode of expression, originally oriental, became by degrees, on account of the schism between Rome and Byzantium, more and more westernized. Concurrently, Catholics became gradually estranged, by their way of life, from all that has been, since the fifteenth century, 'missionary country'.

The Church, as a living organism, possesses a dynamic equilibrium which makes it capable of change, provided that its essential structure is preserved. In so far as the Church, without ceasing to be divine, is a human society, its actual way of life reflects man's ways of thinking and acting. All tradition is not dogma, every custom is not sacrosanct, even if both the one and the other are orthodox and beneficial. New points of view on the Christian mystery, new ways of translating it into life, may make their appearance, and may be the expression of the special characters of persons and peoples.

The missionary, for his part, is marked by the Christian culture of his upbringing, through which he was brought into contact with the Church. By the grace of Christ which it brought him, his thought is illumined by the divine light, his heart inflamed with the love of God; yet his life continues to derive from the experience received in his particular surroundings, for these it was that contributed to his formation as a Christian. It is not that the divine mystery is indistinguishable from its expression in a particular culture, but that there exists between the two a vital bond. For it is the Spirit that teaches the Christian to pray, and even 'prays in him' (Rom. 8: 13, 26-27), and the Spirit that 'pours forth' charity; but the same Spirit expresses himself both by the interior word that is unutterable and by the spiritual experience of the Christian community.

All men are not called to the same forms of prayer or of charity, and these vary according to circumstances. The missionary, in introducing his hearers to the Christian life, relies, above all, on the interior Teacher. Still, he has his own instrumental part to play; and he can do so only by showing, through prayer and example, how he himself understands and lives the life of prayer and charity. In this sphere his attitude, however truly Christian, is, none the less, characteristically European, inasmuch as the life of the Church was for centuries concentrated in Europe, and it is still Europe that provides the majority of missionaries. These are not unaware of the particular and partial character of their way of living the life of Christ, but they have no choice but to start from what they actually are, while fostering in their disciples the development of their own Christian personality.

In general, when the Church makes its appearance in a new country, it comes in all its complex being in which are united, without confusion, its essential divine structure and its human expression. The missionary, penetrated through and through with the European Christian tradition, will have great difficulty in discerning where precisely development is called for, and to what point it is legitimate. Apart from very minor questions, he will be apprehensive lest, in touching one element, he endanger the whole structure, and so compromise his mission. Only the assistance of the Holy Ghost, and the directives and control of the Hierarchy, will enable him to confront with confidence a task demanding much time and patience.

Some, desirous of prompt results, have been led to maintain that the customs of the Christian West were simple excrescences on the tree of life, which is the Church of Christ. If that were so, it would suffice to remove them, to restore to it its authentic appearance. No human disfigurement would then be left to prevent outside peoples from recognizing the Church and giving it their allegiance.

That view comes from thinking of the Church as something discarnate. The Word of God, in his Incarnation, could have taken any human nature; the particular one he took certainly possesses universal significance; and yet the Incarnate Word is still Jesus Christ, the carpenter of Galilee in the first century. It would be quite useless and false to aim at stripping the Son of God of this human garb which is so individual and through which he reveals himself.

In an analogous way, the Church, the body of Christ, transcends all cultures, and none of them is indispensable to it. That does not mean that it excludes them, or that it is indifferent to them, but that it encompasses them without being confused with or limited by them. By taking on one of them, it expresses the inexhaustible mystery of Christ in a new way, one specially appropriate to the people among whom the culture originated. The Church could take up all of them, either in turn or together, but it cannot remain without expressing itself in some way, for, like its Head, it is called to become incarnate, it is sent to speak to mankind.

We do not claim that every word and deed of its members is a true expression of the mystery. They are human and sinful; their thought and life are prone to failings, narrowness, deviations, which the Church works incessantly to correct. Yet, in so far as their life corresponds faithfully to their vocation, they truly exhibit the mystery, without, however, exhausting it completely.

In the countries subject to missionary action Christianity has obviously not yet formed its suitable cultural expression; or else, this expression, though brought to birth, has not reached maturity. Since Christianity must express itself somehow, it can do so, provisionally, only in a foreign culture, that of the missionary.

Peoples and Cultures

This cultural expression of Christianity can only with difficulty be assimilated by the people evangelized, precisely because it is a foreign one. They themselves are penetrated with their own particular culture, in which there is no place for Christ or for his message. On account of the cultural context in which it is presented, they fail to perceive clearly what is the supernatural gift offered by the missionary, and its appearance in their midst seems to cast doubt on their whole manner of life.

To understand properly this situation, we have to recur to the idea of what a culture is and the laws that govern it.

Cultivating a field means inciting nature by some human labour to produce fruits which nature left to itself would be incapable of producing, for what nature left to itself alone produces is 'wild' vegetation. Such a figure gives us an idea of what that culture means in the vocabulary of philosophy, the culture, not of an expanse of soil, but of humanity itself. Man being a spirit animating a body of flesh, his nature in itself is a progressive nature. The labour of reason and the virtues is natural in the sense that it is in conformity with the essential inclinations of human nature; it brings into play the essential springs of human nature. It is not natural in the sense that it is supplied ready made by nature: it is an addition to what nature produces by itself and by itself alone. Nature, no doubt, can also be considered without this labour of

[1] J. Maritain, *Religion and Culture* (Essays in Order, Sheed and Ward, 1931), page 13.

reason, and as reduced therefore to energies of a sensitive order and mere instincts, or considered before this labour of reason, that is to say in a state of, as it were, embryonic involution and absolute primitiveness.

This work, to deserve the name of culture, has to be 'a truly human and therefore mainly intellectual, moral and spiritual[1] development', very clearly, a material and technical development, by the fact that man is an incarnate, not a pure, spirit. Presupposing both nature and the labour of reason, culture ought to keep in the line of nature, but may deviate from that line, allow itself to be sponged upon by *artificialism* contrary to nature and by perversions of varying degrees of gravity.'[2]

This analysis from the standpoint of philosophy agrees with that given by *cultural anthropology*, which is the term used in America to designate the science called elsewhere *ethnology*, and whose terminology is coming to be adopted universally. Anthropology gives this as its technical definition of culture: 'All that part of human behaviour that man has learnt and fashioned himself, and that is handed down as a social tradition, and not in a biological manner.'

Man does not learn to be hungry or sleepy, to shout or to breathe. He does learn to paint his skin, to tint or cut his hair, to clothe himself, to speak, to make and handle tools.

It is as 'natural' for a westerner of the twentieth century to wear a suit as it was for a Chinese, till recent years, to wear a robe. The pronunciation of the English

[1] *Ibid.*, page 14.   [2] *Ibid.*

th, the German *ch*, the Spanish *j*, the French *r*, is as 'natural' to each of these peoples as it is almost impossible to the others. The Chinese eat dog, the Jews abhor pork, the Hindus refuse to eat beef, and the English can never understand how the French can feed on frog's legs. In greeting a friend, the French shake hands, a practice they have taken from the English, who use it more often in greeting strangers; the Arab puts his hand on his forehead, lips and heart.

In short, the manifold counsels and examples man receives from his surroundings inculcate a particular technique of living, which is a more or less successful adaptation to geographical conditions, and also a language, whose structure conveys a certain way of thinking. On these foundations is erected a way of social life, expressing itself in family, economic and political relationships elaborated in the course of history. According as the different family, professional, regional and national groups interpenetrate and are superposed on one another, or are isolated and differentiated, there arise cultures that are widespread or restricted. But, in the strictest sense, the term 'culture' is reserved to the patrimony of a vast social aggregate, that is to say, to an ethnic or national group.

The elements which make up a culture are not set out like goods on the counter of a general store. They support and strengthen one another in forming a whole whose parts are interconnected like cells in a living body, so that any action on one element ultimately affects the whole. The harmony of the various features may be highly subtle and difficult to discern; in fact, the laws of their association are practically unknown at present. What is certain is the existence of a network of powerful links between the different elements, and that is called the law of cultural integration.

To see how it works, let us go over rapidly the problem of clothing, as an example. If man makes clothes for himself, it would seem to be primarily in order to protect himself from the weather; it is a matter of biology. It appears quite natural to cover or uncover oneself according as it is cold or hot. Yet some who live in cold parts, right at the south of America, for example, know no use of clothing; even in tropical countries, the nights can be cold, or slight variations of temperature can easily be dangerous to people unaccustomed to them. It is a fact that, with people who have kept to their ancestral custom of wearing no clothes, colds and congestion of the lungs are frequent, and are among the chief causes of high infant mortality. From this simple point of view, Europeans, whether missionaries or not, have advised them to use clothes. But it has been found that their use has brought with it the development of rickets among the people, since the deficiencies of their diet were no longer compensated by the absorption of sunlight. To counteract this loss, better nourishment should have been provided. The introduction of clothing as a protection against heat and cold was treated as a distinct problem, when it was part of the general problem of organic equilibrium to be viewed as a whole.

Wearing clothes, it is clear, seems to respond to a moral need, that of safeguarding modesty and of protecting against concupiscence. Yet it has been found that their introduction among people who had not used them before did not always favour morality; in fact, it often caused a decline. This may not have been due to the clothes as such, but to those who advocated them, who stopped short at the material aspect of the change, without considering the spirit animating it. In the concrete, morality rests on a received discipline of living, whose structure takes account of the material conditions of life, so that the discipline itself comes ultimately to be expressed in particular attitudes. Against the temptations bound up with the way of life are set up 'taboos', if we like to call them that, or, at any rate, rules of conduct to ensure victory over temptations. Thus, girls and boys are kept strictly separate till the time of marriage, and very severe punishment is inflicted on breaches of marriage-customs; for adultery it is often the death-penalty. Clothing might appear of itself to tell against some kinds of temptation; but, unless it is accompanied with a new attitude of mind, with new practical rules of moral conduct, it is of no effect. On the contrary, its introduction may seem to make the traditional rules unnecessary, and there is a strong risk of their being swept away indiscriminately.

Clothing is due also to social requirements, which indicate perhaps its most essential function, certainly its most despotic one. It gives man his place in society. At all times, and in all countries, certain types of cloth-

ing—reduced perhaps to very little, a cloak, an orna-
ment, etc.—have been reserved to certain classes of
persons. They permit of instantly distinguishing the
soldier from the civilian, the ruling classes from the
masses, or working- from leisure-hours. In the modern
world, which believes in the basic equality of all, differences tend to diminish; but it is still doubtful if we
will arrive, as some hope, at complete uniformity, even
among the same people. To appreciate the scope of
this factor in social life, we have only to imagine the
horror which would be caused by the appearance of a
short skirt at a dinner party at Buckingham Palace, or
of a dinner-jacket at a workers' meeting. Everyone is
aware of the tyranny of fashion. Without going into
the question of principle, we may recognize that it can
easily involve expense that cannot be afforded, clothes
that are uncomfortable or unhealthy, and sometimes
improper, even when ideas and customs have undergone
a normal development.

The question of clothing comes also into the sphere
of religion. Differences of dress according to age, sex,
or occupation are often bound up with the idea that the
life of each individual is a response to a divine vocation,
and their object is to show forth this vocation publicly.
Even in societies as secularized as those of modern
Europe, there still remain traces of this idea in the
clothes worn at baptism, first communion, weddings
and at times of mourning, in the religious habit, in the
wearing of scapulars, or in the use of blue and white as
a sign of consecration to Our Lady, as well as, of course,

in the liturgical vestments. Up to now, the non-western cultures have been more penetrated with the sacred than ours; that is to say, the colours and shapes of clothes are, in them, full of religious significance of a very precise nature. It is impossible to propose any changes without at least seeming to minimize the importance of the beliefs attaching to them, and often of throwing doubt on these in one way or another.

At different periods, and among different peoples, very various kinds of clothes have been adopted in similar circumstances. This shows that their shapes and colours are not necessarily bound up with a fixed social, moral or religious purpose. In fact, however, they are not easily to be separated from the symbolic value attributed to them by common opinion in a given society.

An analysis of other cultural elements would show that they too are intimately related to all the aspects of human life. They form an integral unity, and are organized in an *art of living*, which subsists in a state of dynamic equilibrium; that is to say, the culture assures the continuance through the ages of a settled way of life, expressive of the special character of peoples, while at the same time it is able to adapt itself to a changing world. Slow development may occur without endangering the stability of the whole. Sometimes, however, circumstances arise which confront a people with alien importations of great moment, problems of a special kind, and standpoints at variance with their own; and these menace the very life of their culture. Thus, the barbarian invasions of the Roman Empire, the Islamic

D

conquest of the Near East and North Africa, made a real breach in the continuity of the cultural development of these regions.

The missionary, whose duty is to proclaim the Gospel of Christ, has no intention of upsetting the culture of the people he approaches, for he recognizes it as a normal human development, even though it stands in need of correction in some of its details. The people, though, resent his arrival, and see in it a danger, particularly as his message tends completely to undermine the religious values by which they had been living, which made up the noblest element of their culture, and were, in fact, the principle on which it was organized. Why were the Roman emperors, like the Latin and Greek masses, so violently opposed to the spread of Christianity? It was because they could not conceive how it was possible to reject the gods of the empire or the city without ceasing to be a loyal subject and a good citizen.

A people cannot belong to the Church without effecting a dissociation between the religious elements and the strictly human elements of its culture, in order to engraft the latter on Christ. But this separation appears to be fraught with danger, and the fruitfulness of the graft is not easily seen.

Does this mean that the religious beliefs and practices of non-Christian peoples are totally false? By no means; for God has endowed human nature, in its creation, with an aspiration to the supernatural. A spiritual impulse, aversion from evil, devotion to the service of others, rub shoulders in the heart of every man with selfishness, pride and sensuality. It rests with the individual, aided by grace, to make the former of these tendencies prevail. Grace, too, will never be wanting, for 'it is his [God's] will that all men should be saved, and be led to recognize the truth' (1 Tim. 2: 4).

God has never ceased to make himself known to man. As St Paul tells us, 'from the foundations of the world men have caught sight of his invisible nature, his eternal power and his divineness, as they are known through his creatures' (Rom 1: 20). Therefore, the impious are inexcusable for not having given God their homage and gratitude. Man, being by nature social, is formed, too, by the positive religion of which his culture is the carrier; as this tradition may seem to satisfy his religious needs, it shuts him out, in a corresponding degree, from the fulness of the Light; yet it may help to develop in him some sense of adoration of God, of submission to Providence, of prayer and virtue. In spite of the errors they contain, whether through human infirmity, or through the continual effort of Satan to deform them and make them issue in sinful conduct, the positive religions, as exhibited in actual life,[1] are not completely lacking in value.

In fact, if God gave Israel exclusively the privilege of preparing the way of the Messias, it might be said, in an analogous way, that every people has its own 'sacred history', for, from the beginning, God has been working

---

[1] We leave aside the question of religions taken in the abstract as each a body of doctrines and practical obligations. Religion exists to be lived, and it is of concern to the missionary in that respect alone, for his work is directed not to religions as such, but to the men who live by them.

secretly on men to lead them to the fulness of Revelation. Beyond doubt, there have been persons who have responded to his call, and approached a state of holiness; and the whole people has profited from their influence and example.

The Church has the duty to bring this advance to completion; but it seems at first to disparage it and bring it to a halt. For the missionary has not simply to align himself with a process and carry it to its conclusion, but to correct it and cure its ills, since the stem which is to be grafted on the Church is embedded among evil growths and infected by them.

These various elements, some sound, others dubious or frankly evil, are integrated in a living culture, in which the supernatural and the merely human exist side by side, with the consequent danger of confusion between them. Just as the missionary strives to divest his own actions of any element that is too human, he will not hesitate when charity itself obliges him to upset settled habits if that is necessary for the people to attain to the full measure of supernatural life. Like Christ himself, he must say: 'I have not come to set them aside, but to bring them to perfection' (Mt. 5: 17), but he cannot pass over the complementary assertion: 'I have come to bring a sword, not peace' (Mt. 10: 34).

Preparing men for the Faith

The earliest obstacles to the preaching of the missionary come from the alien character of the Church, and the threat it seems to show towards non-Christian cultures. Fundamentally, what he comes up against derives from the characteristics of human nature, the attachment of people to their ideas and customs, their mistrust of the unknown and the unusual, the fear of possible dangers on venturing into new regions.

In fact, to put one's faith in God is always an adventure of some sort. Abraham, the type of the believer (Rom. 4; Heb. 11), had to face the danger. 'Leave thy country behind thee, thy kinsfolk, and thy father's home', was God's command to him, 'and come away into a land I will shew thee. Then I will make a great people of thee; and I will bless thee' (Gen. 12: 1-2). He had to forgo the tangible security of family ties and of a country with whose resources he was thoroughly acquainted, and stake his life on the impalpable promises of God.

None the less, there are not wanting persons who respond generously to such demands. Abraham 'went out, as the Lord bade him' (Gen. 12: 4), without question or delay. Moses was to display much less promptitude (Exod. 3-4). It requires exceptional strength of character to break one's habits, and an ardent desire for the light to welcome it wherever it appears, and to submit to it entirely.

Every culture, an art of living slowly elaborated in the course of time, has the semblance of a wisdom from which it would be folly to stray. Each generation, admittedly, and every individual, brings a special contribution to it; still their life as a whole bears its strong imprint. No culture, however, is without its imperfections, they arise from the very limitations of the human mind; grievous errors may creep in concerning man's way of life, social relations and religious ideas. In consequence, ways of thought and conduct come to seem normal and good, when they are in fact abominable. No culture is immune from deviations of the sort; and those where the light of God has not yet shone in its fulness, or that refuse to be guided by it, are especially liable to them.

It has to be recognized that the errors integral to a culture and constituting its principles make up an actual counter-teaching. They are much less like a thorn to be extracted than a poison that impairs the mind's aptitude for the truth; and it is truth for which the missionary has to arouse the desire, stimulate the taste, and make the need felt.

For this reason, he must show that he is bound to it with ties that cannot be broken. In his whole attitude, his public and private utterances, he must avoid all pretence, patiently seek exact information, be ready to revise his standpoint in the light of new knowledge obtained, and not to exploit unduly what he already possesses. He will often be drawn to scientific investigation or to the teaching of purely secular matters. This kind of activity gives the Church some incidental prestige, but his real aim is to create an attitude of mind that is one of respect for truth, whether religious or not. He must never allow himself to varnish it for any reason at all; however disconcerting it may appear, he yet places his trust in it. For Christ is subsistent truth; no part of truth is hostile to him, or even alien; it all leads back to him, and, of its own power, counters the virulence of error and destroys it. The intellectual integrity of the missionary is what restores the confidence of the catechumen who, in the light of Christ, feels his world crumbling away; it enables the missionary himself to understand the real aspirations of the people and to provide for them. In fact, it constitutes a secondary motive of credibility for his supernatural message, for one who has a deep regard for truth does not embrace a faith unless he sees it as at least compatible with the truth that all seek.

The contact established in this way helps to arouse curiosity and to make the Church appear in a favourable light, as showing respect for truth; but it is only tenuous, since it reaches man in his intelligence rather than in his totality. The witness so proclaimed is too restricted in scope to remove all hesitation. Man is a creature of emotion as much as of intellect, and, until the heart is won over, the mind finds much difficulty in perceiving what is true, and even more in conforming to its demands. The non-Christian is repelled by the alien, strange character of the Christian message, and instinctively distrusts it. His own religion has been integrated by long tradition with his distinct national way of life, and the missionary comes to assault it. The non-Christian is reluctant to acknowledge that his own culture is gravely defective. Rightly conscious as he is of the human values it contains, which have been fostered by the wisdom of his ancestors, he naturally wonders if they can be retained, and at what cost.

The missionary, then, must be at pains to exhibit the supranational character of the Church. Pope Pius XII in *Evangelii Praecones* said:

> From its beginning to our own day, the Church has always observed the very wise rule by which the Gospel neither destroys nor diminishes anything good, true or beautiful in a people's character and natural genius. In fact, when the Church invites all peoples to ascend, under the guidance of the Christian religion, to a higher form of human culture, it does not act like one who recklessly cuts down a luxuriant forest, plundering and destroying it, but like a man who grafts a fine shoot on a wild growth, and so enables it to produce, later on, fruits no longer bitter but savoury.

The human qualities of peoples are themselves the gift of God, and the missionary, recognizing this, will show them respect, getting to know them, and, in some measure, adapting himself to them. It is of the greatest importance for him to become familiar with the language of the people among whom he works; for that manifests the categories which their minds use, and through these he himself must pass if he is to reach them. Normally, he will conform to the ordinary rules of living, so as not to pass for a boorish person and so lose any hope of a hearing. He may have to adopt the clothes and food of the country. The acquisition of the language is always indispensable,[1] but the adoption

[1] Obviously it could happen that a missionary should do valuable work, even without any knowledge of the language, being prevented for some reason or other from learning it; but such cases are the exception.

of customs demands much good sense and caution. Wholesale imitation, hardly ever desirable, is not always possible, either because it involves danger to health, or because some of the actions of everyday life have a religious significance and so cannot be adopted unreservedly. Any sort of haste is dangerous; there must be time to look about, to understand and form a judgment.

Adaptation is easier in these days, when the various cultures have become connected and tend to some kind of fusion. The missionary no longer arrives in an entirely unknown world, as happened before. We know the labour Father Ricci underwent in the sixteenth century, in gathering reliable information on China. Nowadays, there is an abundance of writings which are easily accessible to the missionary desirous of gaining some idea of the culture he will meet with. His adapting himself to it, though not so necessary in some respects as in others,[1] is a clear sign of his love for the people and his high regard for them.

This attitude may eliminate certain prejudices, but it may fail to impress the people, because to them it appears perfectly normal. The missionary, if he is to gain their affections, must give himself to them, and make use of every opportunity to prove that he really does so. For this reason, the Church puts itself at their service by setting up schools, hospitals, dispensaries, orphanages, reception centres for the victims of catas-

---

[1] Since Asiatics and Africans are often disposed to adopt many European customs, and desire Western culture. However, there are important reservations to be made on this matter; see below, pages 61-2 and 133-8.

trophes, whether arising from nature or man. It sends its missionaries to assist and comfort the poor, defends the victims of injustice, and lends support to efforts to improve living conditions. These are so many various occasions to enter into contact with the people, to acquaint them with the Christian way of life, and make them realize what is meant by the charity that is the gift of the Spirit. The most remarkable instances of these in our day have been the anti-slavery campaign of Cardinal Lavigerie, the work of Father Damien among the lepers in the island of Molokai (Hawaii), the social work of Father Lievens at Chota Nagpur in India, the life led by Charles de Foucauld among the Tuaregs of the Sahara, and the places of refuge set up at Shanghai and Nanking by Father Jacquinot in the very midst of the Sino-Japanese war.

The Church was the first in this field, and, for a long time, the signs of her charity were clear and evident. Nowadays, the various States have largely taken over the direction of these institutions, seeing in them a duty of social justice. In consequence, the spirit animating the Church in so far as she continues that work is less easy to discern, and so it is more urgently necessary to make evident in it the charity that is not opposed to justice, but animates it and goes beyond it. These works would be useless, if they were not properly executed; they require a competent personnel and an established organization. Yet they are not an end in themselves; they are always subordinate to the apostolic work as a whole, and may not monopolize its resources.

Above all, they must be infused with charity, and so exempt from commercialism, competition, and the spirit of bureaucracy.   A Catholic hospital, for example, is not to be valued for the excellence of its equipment, the money it brings in, the exact observation of a time-table, the cures effected, the wonderful operations carried out, nor even for the number of patients who ask for and receive Baptism.   Charity does not claim anything as its right; it does not judge works by their results, even their apostolic ones; it serves according to its ability, in a purely disinterested way.   These are the conditions in which it bears witness to God, and opens to him the hearts of men.

Preaching the Word of God

Under the influence of the Holy Ghost, the Good Tidings, of which the missionary is the herald, is able of itself to gain entrance to the mind and heart of man.

We do not read of St Paul engaging in all sorts of preliminary activities before proclaiming salvation by Christ to the inhabitants of Iconium, Lystra, or Philippi (Acts 14 and 16).   Only once, so it seems, when he had to explain himself at Athens, did he take as his starting-point the traditional beliefs of his hearers (Acts 17). The failure of that approach taught him a lesson, and at Corinth he decided to go straight to the point: 'Christ . . . sent me to preach the gospel; not with an orator's cleverness, for so the cross of Christ might be robbed of its force. . . . When God shewed us his wisdom, the world, with all its wisdom, could not find its way to God; and now God would use a foolish thing, our preaching, to save those who will believe in it. Here are the Jews asking for signs and wonders, here are the Greeks intent on their philosophy; but what we preach is Christ crucified; to the Jews, a discouragement, to the Gentiles, mere folly; but to us who have been called, Jew and Gentile alike, Christ the power of God, Christ the wisdom of God. So much wiser than men is God's foolishness; so much stronger than men is God's weakness' (1 Cor. 1: 17-25).

Likewise, St Francis Xavier, when he evangelized the Indies and Japan, put his whole trust in God. His preparation consisted solely in learning by heart a rough translation of prayers, the Commandments, and a shortened catechism. The rest he left to God, and his very life seems to have been a powerful witness. A Japanese bonze declared that Xavier 'had been unable to explain the Christian teaching owing to his ignorance of Japanese, but that nevertheless his mere presence, his face, his character, his obvious sanctity, preached better than words the truth of his message'.[1]

Yet his results were meagre, especially in Japan. We must admit the evident truth that, so long as certain forms of prejudice remain, it is only too likely that the people, as a whole, will be impervious to the divine Word. Xavier, 'good servant' of God that he was, never forgot that he had to make use of the 'talents' entrusted to him (Mt. 25: 14-30), and did not neglect

[1] J. Broderick, *Saint Francis Xavier*, (Burns Oates, 1952) p. 385.

to draw up plans of action. He learnt from experience that patient preliminary work is normally indispensable.

In any case, it falls to the missionary to proclaim the Christian message as soon as the soil appears ready for it. The task is a difficult one. For the faith, expressed in propositions about divine truth, has the appearance of a clear-cut system; and, further, it demands adherence to a person, that of Christ. Now Christ is not to be adapted; he is to be received either as he is, or not at all.

Besides, the main elements have to be sketched in a language all can understand. It is a problem similar to that of devising a method of education which will transmit to the young the ancestral wisdom expressed in all kinds of ways of thinking and acting. This involves the learning of words and gestures unknown to the child, but, if it is to succeed, it should be based on his own natural gestures and his native or acquired knowledge. In preference to forms, which are variable, principles should be instilled, and these are quite compatible with a spontaneous kind of reaction. Some sort of discipline is inevitable, but education consists essentially in the use of appropriate exterior action to stimulate interior progress; it calls for a communication between master and pupil that enables the former to teach something new in a way that the pupil can understand.

The missionary has to gain a 'hearing' for his message, that is for the Gospel in its fulness, and for all that is closely bound up with the life of the Church. He has at his disposition a language that has been developed over a long period, but which is, for that very reason, all the more mysterious for those outside. He will hardly find in the language of the country equivalent terms which will not be misleading, particularly as in the beginning he will know it only slightly, and grasp very imperfectly the scope of the ordinary religious terms. He will have to put his trust in an interpreter, who may have little familiarity with Christian terminology.

A typical example of this is the experience of St Francis Xavier with his beloved Paul Anjiro, the 'first fruit of Japan'. On the information of the latter, he took *Dainichi* to be the true God, introduced the term into his catechism, and proclaimed himself the restorer of the true worship of *Dainichi*. This gained him a considerable welcome from the Buddhist bonzes, especially those of the Shingon sect, enthusiastic for this unexpected recruit. In reality, the *Dainichi*, the Great Sun, the Enlightener, had nothing in common with a personal, creative God; it was a frankly pantheistic myth, bound up, too, in the popular mind, with obscene imagery. It took Xavier a year to realize that he had been side-tracked; and then, warned by his converts, he put a few precise questions to the bonzes, and was completely undeceived; but it meant the loss of all contact with the Buddhist monasteries. From then on, he preferred the safest course and transcribed in Japanese the Christianized Latin word, *Deus*.

Ricci, when he came up against the same problem, had time to get to know the classical Chinese writers before deciding on a solution. The traditional terms of *Tien*, for 'Heaven', and *Shang-ti*, for 'Lord on high', seemed to him pure enough in meaning to convey the true idea of God. This view of his, however, was not above criticism, for Chu-hi had, in the twelfth century, revised the Confucian teaching in a materialistic sense, and from that time his interpretation was the standard one. Certainly, that was one of the most fiercely contested questions in the only too celebrated *Dispute on the Rites*. To prevent any possible doubt, the Holy See finally insisted on the use of the term *Tien-chu*, the Lord of Heaven.

This expression was at any rate in conformity with the genius of the language. So long as the language is imperfectly known, it could be dangerous to make use of its religious vocabulary to express specifically Christian ideas. But the process of importing Latin words involves creating neologisms that sound strange to the people of the country, or else are somewhat infelicitous in their connections. Many such examples are given by Father de Nobili,[1] whose ideas were much the same as those of Ricci: thus, *missa*, Mass, transcribed into Tamil, was confused with *mixei*, which means 'moustache'.

Whatever the terms adopted, they have to be explained, and so the native language has to be employed. Some of the ideas it conveys offer a starting-point for understanding Christian truth, with which

[1] *Apologie de 1610*, ed., Dahmen, Paris, Desclée de Brouwer, Museum Lessianum, 1924.

they have some similarity. Thus, most religions record interventions of God in history, and these, however remote from the mystery of the Incarnation, may serve to introduce it. Similarly, the *compassionate love* of the Buddhists is a sort of prefiguration of Christian charity.

This procedure, however, has its dangers. In Tamil, for instance, heaven is sometimes represented as the *svarga*, which is a place of carnal delights. In other words, incompatible terms are too hastily taken to mean the same thing. Even when there does exist some analogy, it can have an effect opposite to that intended, blunting the precision of the doctrine in question, and dissembling the original character of the mystery. The fact is that words have no existence independently of a context of imagery, historical background, particular situations, literary associations, in short, of all that goes to make a living language. It is a language of that sort that has to be employed to convey the Christian message, and its transposition for the purpose demands considerable study and a fine discernment.

Altogether, the problem will be solved only when the language has become a mediator, that is to say common to both the Church and the people. The use of European expressions is not bad in itself; it may be found, provisionally, indispensable to preserve the original character of the faith, but requires a suitable commentary to make clear its meaning, and, in consequence, the use of the native tongue. Since, however, the terms which this contains are not in themselves appropriate to convey the divine mystery in its fulness, they have to be developed further and purified.

It is of the highest importance to give a clear sense that the truths of revelation, though expressed in familiar language, are yet absolutely original and transcendent. The Christian message is not to be assimilated to any culture whatever; on the contrary, it is the culture that has to be assimilated to the message.

For this purpose, the missionary has to apply himself to enter into the culture of the people, and even to live according to it in so far as it is sound, in order to share its spirit; he must start from within if he is to translate it properly into Christian terms. He has to smooth the way, helped by his converts or even by non-Christians, and he will not hesitate to revise the current terminology in the interests of precision.[1] The privilege of bringing the work to its conclusion belongs to the indigenous clergy, profiting by the experience of the universal Church.

Finally, it must be emphasized, the technical side of the question is only secondary; the important thing is to live the mystery, in continuous loving contemplation of it. It is then that the Spirit gives the deepest understanding of it and of how various external forms can be used to express it.

[1] Thus in China the persons of the Trinity were long designated by the terms *Pa-té-lé* for the Father, *Fei-lo* the Son, and *Sé-pi-li Tuosan-tuo* the Holy Ghost. Latterly, these barbaric transliterations have been replaced by *Cheng-fou*, *Cheng-tse*, and *Cheng-chen*.

The Life to be Fostered

If the faith were merely a system of truths to be acknowledged, the work of the missionary would stop at this point, having achieved its purpose. But the faith cannot be obtained by human action, it is wholly the gift of God; and, moreover, it remains 'unformed' so long as it does not bring about a change of life, that is to say, *conversion*. Its normal completion is achieved only when it is lived in hope and charity. The faith has to be put forward for acceptance, but the Church's mission is to bring forth people to the supernatural life, and to illuminate their ordinary life in its every aspect by the divine light.

Whenever, in a hitherto non-Christian country, a few come forward under the influence of grace, and receive Baptism, the seed of the Gospel may be said to have ripened; a new Church has been born. It still has to grow and become strong, so as to be capable of renewing the whole people, and recreating them according to the image of God.

Since adherence to the faith has for its effect a change of life, man's progress towards Christ may be retarded or held up, not only by previous religious habits, but by the whole network of his personal and social manner of living.

Undoubtedly, God found, in the past, 'men of good will' in all peoples, and formed them to a virtuous life in a hidden fashion, as he formed Job the Idumaean.

None the less, they are no more immune from back-sliding than are Christians themselves, or they may simply hold back in face of the further steps to which God calls them.

However anxious they may be to obey God without reserve, their conscience is yet darkened, to some extent, by the ideas current around them. This is not to imply that Christians vaunt themselves to be the only posses-sors of the moral law. St Paul, in fact, reproached Greeks as well as Jews for their vices, precisely because they had 'the just decree of God before their minds' that 'those who so live are deserving of death; not only those who commit such acts, but those who countenance such a manner of living' (Rom. 1 : 32). The same idea is expressed by St Francis Xavier, when he declares that

Long before the law came from China to Japan,[1] the Japanese knew that it was wrong to kill, to steal, to bear false witness; their remorse of conscience was a sign of the evil they committed; that is because the duty of refraining from evil and doing what is good is written in the hearts of men. People, therefore, know the com-mandments of God without being taught them by any-one unless it be the Creator of mankind.[2]

It is well known to missionaries that there is no people entirely ignorant of the moral law; here and there, a few wise men attained a high level of doctrine, which

[1] On the admission of the Japanese themselves, Francis Xavier realized that it was to China that they owed, in large measure, their religious inspiration.

[2] *Epistolae S. Francisci Xaverii*, ed. Schurhammer, Rome, Monu-menta Historica S.J., 1944-1945, vol. II, p. 262.

served to regulate the general conduct of their people. Is it possible, then, for a society to discover for itself the natural moral law in its entirety? This would appear doubtful, in view of the profound effects of original sin. The mind of man is still capable of distinguishing good from evil, but, in the absence of light from a higher source, he vacillates and is easily led astray when it comes to deciding what is, in fact, good and what is bad; thus, in many peoples, suicide is held to be required by honour. Moreover, under the impulses of concupiscence, man comes to let his desires prevail over his principles and to make his weakness the measure of right; this explains, for example, the appearance of divorce and polygamy in some societies. This tendency is so strong that it prevails even where divine revelation has been accepted; and we see the nations of Europe, in spite of their long Christian history, legalizing divorce and social injustice.

The rules of life expressed in a country's law and institutions are an exact reflection of its moral climate. Obviously, this does not rule out the possibility that men, through the action of grace and by their own unsullied vision, may preserve their rectitude of conscience, even in surroundings more or less decadent. Yet they are in constant danger from the pressure of opinion of judging modes of action to be normal and good, when they are intrinsically immoral.

Even when the principles adopted by a society are good, it remains to be seen how far they are actually conformed with. It is one thing to know the moral law, and another thing to live up to it, and there may be considerable divergence between the law that is acknowledged and the life that is led. What constitutes a departure from the ideal may make its appearance and become an accepted practice; and people are far more impressed by what they see in actual life than by rules that remain a dead letter. Here, too, Christians themselves are, unfortunately, a case in point. At various periods, numbers of them, swayed by their environment, gave up the sacraments, contemned the laws of marriage, and acquired wealth by violent means. By the same kinds of influence, non-Christians may come to lose the sense of God and of the virtues traditional to their race.

Consequently, morality is in need of help and correction both in its prescriptions and in its practice. 'Christ alone is the guardian of human justice,' wrote Pius XII in the encyclical, *Evangelii Praecones*; and the Church alone maintains it integrally, because she alone is indefectible. She alone provides the means of living constantly faithful to it, for she has the privilege of dispensing the grace of Christ, which alone can assure such fidelity and raise men up again after their repeated falls. She points out what is right in ideas and conduct, and, in doing so, restores the natural bases essential to the being and development of the Christian life. Furthermore, by the theological virtues of faith, hope and charity, the moral life is set on a higher plane of development; the rules already known and lived by are further refined, the conscience made more delicate in its perceptions, and the charity of Christ breaks down all the ramparts of human selfishness.

The world of men, for the most part, ignores the call to this life; for, in spite of its thirst for God, it is, in one of its aspects, an invisible 'world', the world of 'darkness' (Jn. 1 : 5), the world of which Satan is the 'prince' (Jn. 12 : 31; Lk. 4 : 6), and Satan wars against Christ to keep his empire intact, or, at least, to delay its destruction. He is ever active in raising up new adversaries to the Church, and finds ready auxiliaries in that concupiscence which enslaves man to the goods of this world, and the pride which leads him to trust entirely to his own judgment.

The Church, on the other hand, testifies that 'God so loved the world that he gave up his only-begotten Son, so that those who believe in him may not perish, but have eternal life. When God sent his Son into the world, it was not to reject the world, but so that the world might find salvation through him. For the man who believes in him there is no rejection; the man who does not believe is already rejected; he has not found faith in the name of God's only-begotten Son' (Jn. 3 : 16-18). The Church insists that 'we have an everlasting city, but not here; our goal is the city that is one day to be' (Heb. 13 : 14).

It is absolutely indispensable to strive with every possible means to preserve all peoples, or disengage them, from those pernicious teachings that make the enjoyment of this world's goods the sole end of man in this life. . . . It is absolutely imperative to teach all that we are here in exile making for our true country which is immortal (Pius XII, *Evangelii Praecones*).

Between Satan and the Church there is no possible compromise. Man must make his choice; it is a question of life or death for eternity. 'Rejection lies in this, that when the light came into the world, men preferred darkness to light; preferred it, because their doings were evil. Anyone who acts shamefully hates the light, will not come into the light, for fear that his doings will be found out. Whereas the man whose life is true comes to the light, so that his deeds may be seen for what they are, deeds done in God' (Jn. 3: 19-21).

There is no need to disguise the fact that, in the beginning, the unusual aspect, and more or less alien character, of the Church may hinder or delay the people among whom it is set up from drawing near to Christ, but that is only a secondary obstacle. The real one is men's attachment to sin; the barrier causing them to stumble in their advance consists of the formidable demands on them that Christianity entails; these they well understand, and too often they hang back. The best of them are liable to repeat the experience of the rich young man (Mt. 19: 16-22). He had kept the commandments from his youth, and, urged on by the desire to ascend further, he fell at the feet of Jesus, asking him what he should do. When he learnt that he should abandon everything, he became sad and discouraged. In a sense, the non-Christian, too, is called to sacrifice all his goods to gain the pearl of great price (Mt. 13: 45-46).

The Gospel has a real power of attraction, its beauty is striking, and many recognize its truth. Many, also, hesitate to 'take the step', because their principles and habits of life would be overthrown. Men's actions, when exposed to the brilliance of the divine light, change their colour; the change, in some cases, may be imperceptible, but, elsewhere, it is a violent one. Benevolence must become charity; forgiveness of injuries, which might seem foolish or bad, becomes of obligation; divorce and polygamy, which might seem to be natural, must be abolished; the sense of family responsibility, while remaining alert, must yet allow for a proper appreciation of the religious vocation; and moral value does not reside in external conduct, but in the internal attitude.

Before the word of God made itself heard, the life of men ran, calm and clear, in well-defined channels; and, all at once, the dykes grow weak and break at the impact of a torrent that sweeps men away indiscriminately. Previously, they knew where they were going, they could count up their possessions; but when, in obedience to grace, they go over to Christ, they are, indeed, aware that they are offered wealth of quite a different kind, but as yet they have no experience of it; they cannot foresee precisely how far their life will be transformed by it.

The particular attachments keeping them away from Christ vary with the individual, and must be studied in each several case. One factor, however, is common to all; there is a counter attraction to what the Church offers, not only in the passions and habits of the individual, but also in the pressure of the world and public opinion. There must be an endeavour to nullify this, or even to reverse the trend. Thereby, the Church is brought to intervene in temporal problems with which it is not directly concerned; and, in addition, it has to develop its own organizations to give effective support to all Christians, whether newly converted or of long standing. In this way, it can gradually transform a non-Christian into a Christian environment, without which conversion must entail real heroism, and so be restricted to a small number; the local Church, then, would never be able to grow to its normal dimensions.

3

INTERFERENCE
OF TEMPORAL FACTORS

SINCE the Church is wholly a mystery of the supernatural order, her essential mission is a supernatural
one. But, since she cannot accomplish it without
being 'incarnated' in a manner analogous to the
Incarnation of Christ, her Head, her influence penetrates
deeply into the temporal[1] order.

The Son of God was made man; he acted in human
fashion, 'fashioned in the likeness of men' (Phil. 2: 7).
Consequently, he was confronted with typically human
problems. It is true that he took care to uphold the
supernatural character of his mission, and refused to
take sides in purely temporal questions, as in a dispute
over an inheritance (Lk. 12: 13), or that of the tax
imposed by the Roman authorities (Mt. 22: 15). The
Sanhedrin might accuse him before Pilate of political
designs, but the false witnesses were their own refuta-
tion, for Christ never taught disobedience to the laws
or to established authority.

---

[1] This term is open to ambiguity. It is ordinarily opposed to
'spiritual', and, in that way, indicates the material side of human
life. In itself it is applicable to all that is essentially subject to time,
and so may comprise the whole of human life in so far as directed
to temporal ends. This is the sense in which it is used here, in
opposition, that is, to 'supernatural'.

Christ's mission itself required him to correct many of the ideas current in his day. If, for example, the possession of riches is not wrong in itself, it is yet dangerous, through encouraging the growth of earthly desires (Mt. 19: 24). Foresight and skill in temporal business may indeed be commendable, but trust in Providence is better (Mt. 6: 25). Authority, whether domestic or political, has a right to obedience; but it is not supreme (Lk. 14: 26; Jn. 19: 11). Revenge, though permitted by the law of Moses, is henceforth forbidden (Mt. 5: 39), and the same applies to divorce (Mt. 5: 32; 19: 9). We must love even our enemies (Mt. 5: 44), and the attitude of Christ to the Samaritans (Jn. 4; Lk. 9: 55) is an actual indication how intolerable to him was racial hatred.

He was equally forthright in his treatment of existing customs, such as the observance of the Sabbath (Mk. 2: 27; Mt. 12: 11); the frequent washings (Mt. 15: 3); the practice of fasting (Mt. 9: 15); the buying and selling in the temple (Jn. 2: 15; Mt. 21: 12).

In this way, he brought back law and life to a state of purity; but, at the same time, his action affected the Jewish culture of his day in its principles and practices, which were in an imperfect, even a perverted, condition. In general, when principles are restored to vigour and attitudes set up correspondingly, the wider and deeper their reach the more the balance of social life is endangered. 'Nor is new wine put into old wine-skins; if that is done, the skins burst, and there is the wine spilt and the skins spoiled. If the wine is new, it is put into fresh wine-skins, and so both are kept safe' (Mt. 9: 17). The comparison must not be pressed to prove that Christ desired to set up an entirely new culture; but it does mean that cultural elements must be radically reshaped if they are to form part of a higher synthesis.

Likewise, the Church, knowing that her mission is a supernatural one, refrains from taking over the management of temporal matters. As human beings, her members have to take their normal part in society. Those, however, with responsibilities in the strictly ecclesiastical sphere will normally decline to take on temporal functions in addition, on account of the confusions inevitably occasioned; though, in exceptional conditions, there may be good reasons for combining the two. The Church, as such, is never involved therein. She leaves all, Christians or not, free to choose their form of government and of social and family relationships. When she became a predominant force in the Roman Empire, she did not agitate for the replacement of one ruler by another, for national liberties, for the legal suppression of slavery, or for fresh legislation on domestic matters.

Her contribution is quite other than a recasting of temporal society; it is the divine life, an interior principle of personal renovation. The virtues of faith, hope and charity bring light of a higher order to bear on the whole moral life of man; and the whole of life becomes thereby capable of being raised to the supernatural level. 'In eating, in drinking, in all that you do, do everything as for God's glory', was the teaching of St Paul (1 Cor. 10: 31). What is required for a meal to become a supernatural act? It is that man should live by the light of grace, and should have a right intention; and this, in turn, supposes that the act should be in accord with the moral law, and the outcome of a general will to live for God. It matters little what the food in question is; everyone is free to follow his inclinations. The Church may intervene, and at times does so; for example, to instil in her members a certain idea of asceticism, to some degree indispensable, she enjoins days of fasting and abstinence, and these have their own reaction on the life of society.

In a more general way, the Church's penetration of the temporal sphere comes about through the close connection between theology and morals on the one hand, and morals and techniques on the other. We have already analysed the way in which divine revelation revivifies the moral law, and there is no need to return to the subject, but the second point needs examination.

Man being a spiritual being, free and immortal, there is no aspect of human life to which moral considerations are irrelevant. No doubt, the economic and juridical orders have their own particular autonomy, since they have their specific ends and follow their proper laws. The economic order is that of the relations of man to nature (in the material sense); it regulates the exploitation of material resources and their distribution, and is governed by laws such as those of supply and demand. The juridical order comprises the relations

between persons within society; it secures the co-opera-
tion of each to the good of the whole, and, to this end,
has to determine the extent of individual rights and
duties. In both, what is established is a technique of
life on this earth; but, since they are both concerned
with human persons, they cannot leave out of all con-
sideration the question of eternal destiny. Hence any
use of immoral means is ruled out—in principle, if not
always in fact—even if such bring technical advantages;
and it follows, too, that the supreme end of the economic
and juridical orders is to ensure that justice prevails in
the human relations with which they are concerned.
All this follows from their essential subordination to
the moral order. This latter, in its turn, has for its
object the direction of man to his final end, and so is
subordinated to religion, in which God, the final End,
makes known his summons, his demands, and the means
of salvation he puts at our disposition.

If, then, it is no part of the Church's business to determine what economic and juridical arrangements are
most suitable to a given temporal situation, it does fall
to her to draw the attention of the various societies to
the moral principles that should govern their whole
activity, and to urge their detailed application, while
leaving to each society the responsibility of working
out the best practical arrangements. In these matters
she acts, not directly, but by setting forth obligations
and urging their fulfilment, at one and the same time
stating the true principles and stirring up her members
to adapt their lives to them without waiting for the

reform of institutions, useful or indispensable though that may be.

A characteristic example of this is the attitude of the early Church towards slavery. Neither the apostles nor their successors inveighed against the inhuman character of that institution. They did not hesitate to affirm that slaves ought to obey their masters, and that, in doing so, they were obeying God himself, and so they ought to put their hearts into it, and not merely serve with their bodies. But, at the same time, masters were taught it was their duty to God to treat their slaves in a humane fashion, since these were equally children of the same Father, servants of the same Master, God, with whom 'there is no respect of persons' (Eph. 6: 5-9; Col. 3: 22-4: 1; 1 Pet. 2: 18-25). A new principle had been introduced, the 'revolutionary' principle of the equality of all men before God. It only needed that Christians should begin to grasp this idea and live accordingly, for the system to be undermined and marked for collapse. The force of their example and later of their teaching would one day lay low the institutional structure from which the spirit had already been put to flight. But we can see that it was the whole life of the Roman Empire that was rendered unstable, for slavery was a most important factor in social relations and economic production. Both of these, therefore, had to be recast, and new forms devised, and this gave rise to unrest and obloquy. No doubt, the people of Rome distorted the facts when they spread the rumour that the Christians were stirring up the slaves to revolt; but they were not mistaken in their view that the Church was introducing the germ of a radical social change.

In many other questions, too, the Church manifests principles, and teaches behaviour, opposed to established practice. The scandal it thereby occasions is no less than that of the faith itself, and is inherent to it. No 'adaptation' or human prudence can avail to eliminate it, unless the Church betrays itself and the integrity of its mission.

Mingling of Cultures

At the level we have considered, the intervention of the Church in the temporal sphere is a direct consequence of its mission, and is not just an example of contact between one culture and another. The moral principles which, by the light of revelation, it restores to vigour, are not the appanage of a particular culture, but should be an inspiration common to all; they are not alien to anyone, but natural to every man, though by many they are only dimly, if at all, perceived.

Yet the Church, besides the mysterious, supernatural influence it exerts on men, also speaks to them by its missionaries. The heralds of Christ are themselves human beings, with habits of mind and action that are doubtless Christian, but form only one way, among many other possible ones, of living as a Christian; they bear, too, the imprint of a particular culture, in these days generally a Western one. It is not easy, either for the missionary or his audience, to distinguish the universal, 'Catholic', principles of which he is the bearer, from the cultural expression they take on with him. Thus there is a close connection, in fact not by right, between the moral contribution of the Church and the cultural contribution of the missionary. Hence, we have another source of interventions in the temporal sphere, due, this time, not to the nature of the Church as a whole, but to the character of a local Church; and these interventions are subject, at least in part, to the general laws of 'acculturation'.

A culture, as we have already seen, is in a state of dynamic equilibrium, that is to say, it is both stable and in continuous movement. Each member of a society is moulded by the language and customs inherited from his forbears; these provide a vision of the world, a way of confronting problems, a manner of life, characteristic of that particular culture. Since it is men who are moulded by it, a culture cannot be simply imposed; it is an education that should bring each person to accept it freely, leaving him free to inquire as to its value, and to introduce modifications. What the individual brings in this way, far from conflicting with the culture, is itself an expression of it, and a fulfilment of its potentialities for living. Wisdom and culture, being human, are never perfect, but grow in perfection through a long series of tentative experiments. It is a part of wisdom to have a general trust in the cultural heritage which embodies ancestral experience, but it would be foolish to think that all problems have been solved in advance and definitively. A culture, then, develops chiefly through the influence of 'pioneers', even though a spontaneous

F

reaction of self-defence holds back the premature com-
mitment of the whole group to new ways, as yet un-
tried and uncertain in their issue. It is rather like the
action of a bather who feels the water first with his
finger to see if it is not too cold. The finger in this
case consists of the disciples, the pioneers of the new
way.

Pressure from within is combined with the action of
an external force of cultural development, the impact
of one culture on another, and this sets before each of
them the problem of its own peculiar value, and brings
about certain changes in each; this is what is known as
'*acculturation*'. It arises as soon as a 'foreigner', one
formed in another culture, comes into contact with a
given society. As a rule, such a one has no intention
of introducing any change at all in the life of those
around him; he lives in his own way, without troubling
about other people, or else adopts from free choice the
customs of the place. Yet he is bound to lead people
to question these. His way of greeting or of eating, of
going about his affairs or decorating his house, are
different from what is customary. Even if he takes pains
to do 'like everyone else', his manner lacks assurance,
he makes mistakes, and so indicates, without being aware
of it, the existence of different habits. This is quite
enough to suggest to the people of the country that their
ways are not 'natural', but derived from tradition;
other attitudes are seen to be possible, and some of them
may appear better adapted to deal with this or that
problem of living. This is what we mean when we say

a man 'leaves his mark' on his surroundings, and they on him.

If the foreigner is a single person, and if, besides, he has little contact with the natives, the problem to which his coming gives rise may pass unnoticed. But if there are many of them, and they include men of distinction, forceful men, who attract the notice of people, there is brought about a *situation of contact* between the two cultures. They become interdependent, and the effects of this vary according to the form and duration of the contact, and also according to the degree of receptivity or resistance of the members of the two groups.

It is sometimes imagined that, once the contact has been broken off or greatly restricted in scope, each culture would simply return to its original state. According to this view, the cultures of Asia or Africa, once they recover their political independence and their freedom to order their future as they please, will abandon that western culture which affected them for a time, regardless of their own wishes, and will renew their bonds with their own past to develop according to their natural genius.

Obviously, every people has its own special character, and tends to uphold it. It is equally clear that accession to political independence goes along with a strong aspiration to be 'themselves', in every sphere of life. But these values, at one time 'foreign'—western, in the present case—have penetrated the cultures in question more deeply than was at first suspected. They have been tried, and the experiment has left lasting effects, in proportion to its own duration. Just as the human organism, after taking medicine or poison, remains permanently affected, and reacts to outside influences in a way different from before, so contact between two cultures leaves a permanent imprint on each of them. Once the first impulse of ill humour or self-assertiveness has passed, an impulse to discard all foreign elements, the peoples become aware that these elements are already partly assimilated to their own native culture. The task that then awaits them is to sift all the elements at hand and reject what seems definitely opposed to their own genius as well as those aspects of their own past that are evidently defunct. The way is thus opened up towards a new and original synthesis based on both cultures.

Under the influence of acculturation, the development of a society may work itself out by slow, almost imperceptible degrees. Thus, Ricci in China, and de Nobili in India, with their successors, opened up long ago new horizons to the people of those countries, introducing to them ideas which made their way by gradual infiltration.

Development may also proceed with the speed of revolution. That will be the case especially when one of the two cultures in contact is seen to be manifestly superior to the other in a sphere of vital importance, for this produces a violent effect. Even if the people so touched on a sensitive place in regard to their culture continue to hold theirs to be superior in other respects, their relative inferiority is still felt to be intolerable. An instinct of self-defence moves them to refuse to acknowledge it, to adopt an ostrich-like attitude. The feeling of inferiority remains hanging over them, and brings into being pioneer-spirits who devote themselves to restoring the balance by assimilating those cultural elements that are the strong points of the other people. They themselves are liable to go to excess, to despise their own past, and to try to incorporate the foreign culture in its entirety. In any case, the traditional culture is disrupted, its elements tend to fall apart and to be transformed under the impact of new forces. The balance will be restored, once the native genius of the people has effected a symbiosis of its own, at once rooted in the past and incorporating new elements from outside.

It is impossible to understand the missionary problems of the present time without realizing that a strong revolutionary ferment is at work among the peoples, not only politically but also culturally. The Church itself, in fact, brings to them a ferment of renewal, which may act slowly, or else, in cases where their culture is at marked variance with the principles of natural morality, may cause a sudden upheaval. Doubtless, the effect of the impact of the Church's supernatural contribution is more profound than any other factor, but, since here its action is essentially interior and the means invisible, it is all the more difficult to assess its temporal results; these are, on the one hand, retarded by human sinfulness, and, on the other, being due to an inner change rather than an external agency, may come to be confused with the natural development of the culture.

Besides, in our own day, missionary expansion and

western penetration have, in fact, coincided. Availing herself of her scientific and technical discoveries, Europe, in the course of the nineteenth century, extended her political and cultural influence all over the globe. In so doing, she started a revolution in ways of living, and spread abroad ideas that are far as yet from having realized all their consequences. There is no essential connection between this action in the temporal sphere and missionary action, but they are connected in time. They operate at different levels; yet, inasmuch as the missionary, too, exerts secondarily a cultural influence, this becomes, in fact, conjoined with that resulting from western penetration. The actual development of the Asiatic and African cultures is prompted by both these agencies, and is complicated by their own independent reaction to them. Nothing is harder than to distinguish the effect proper to each of these factors, and it is doubtful if that can ever be done adequately. The result remains common to all; but the important thing is to define on which scale the action of the missionary should lean, if he is to be faithful to his essential task, and what are the temporal obstacles before him.

The Church and Family Life

The family, being the natural sphere in which man develops, and to which he is most strongly bound by affection, often forms an important factor in his adhesion to, or rejection of, Christ. It is by no means rare for a whole family to be converted after one of its members.

What is hardest for a catechumen is to go against the opinion of his family, when it remains firmly hostile. It irks man to live in solitude. When he is cut off from his family, he feels uprooted, but, with the support of the family, he is ready to face anything.

Whenever the family is based on the natural law of monogamy and indissolubility, the Church has only to strengthen its unity by a public expression of approval and by bringing the faithful to the sacrament of matrimony. It is, obviously, quite possible for a society to have kept this tradition of the natural character of marriage; the studies of Schmidt seem to show that this was the case with the African pygmies. But in many peoples divorce or polygamy, or both, have been rife, though the forms and rules in vogue vary considerably.

The introduction of polygamy was not always due to the same causes. It may arise from sexual licence and a tendency to look upon women as a mere object of pleasure, in which case it is generally a luxury that only the rich can afford. It would, however, seem rare to find this cause alone at work; nearly always, especially when the custom is widespread, motives of a higher order are present.

To take a wife is to enter into a union with her family. It is, therefore, an excellent way of settling long-standing disputes, or of sealing an 'offensive and defensive' alliance; it is a pledge of security and progress for the two families concerned. In monarchical regimes, princesses were often thus disposed of for political reasons. But even in the West, the centralization of political power is something quite recent, and elsewhere it is far from being achieved. As long as families retain a large measure of autonomy, and have to rely on their own resources for their protection, a network of matrimonial alliances is a vital necessity; and this is made possible by a plurality of wives. Polygamy is thus a source of family power.

Often it is also a source of wealth. Nearly all peoples, at least in their beginnings, had a spontaneous impulse to set up a relationship between the fecundity of women and that of the soil. This idea, a religious one, is seen at work in the numerous feminine divinities to whom was attributed the patronage of agriculture, and in the custom of reserving certain special agricultural tasks to women, in some cases to virgins. In parts of Africa, up to the present time, the cultivation of the fields is reserved to women; men take it on only with reluctance, or in certain special circumstances. Where the soil is poor and its cultivation takes much time and toil, it takes up a woman's whole time, and another is needed to fetch water, collect wood, do the cooking, etc. A catechumen may well argue that, if he dismissed one of his wives, he could not go on living. When conditions are less severe, the possession of many wives may not be indispensable, but is always an advantage.

The importance of this factor is seen in the persistence, even the advance, of polygamy in North Africa, in spite of the growth of Christianity, the attraction of western modes of life, and the protests of young men who find it difficult to marry. The reason is that contact with foreigners had multiplied the economic value of women. Formerly, all they had to do was to assure a supply of the ordinary necessities. Then came European traders, bought certain kinds of fruit, and expressed their desire to buy as much as could be obtained. The price they paid may have been ridiculously low, but they did pay, and the natives found themselves in possession of unknown, undreamt-of wealth. To increase this, plantations had to be extended, and more wives acquired. They were thus the essential springs of the economic machinery; they produced the fruit, which brought in the money, which purchased additional wives. In addition, the wife bore children, some of them girls, who began by helping with the work of the fields, and could later be sold for a good price; in every way, then, she was the chief source of profit. As a result, the marriage agreement, which used to be an exchange of gifts between two families as a sign of their alliance, tends to become a contract of sale, or at least of hire, and may reach an exorbitant sum.[1] The attraction of wealth is so strong that missionaries have often to rebuke their Christian people both for taking many wives and for selling their daughters to married men; and young men, unable to afford the payment demanded, are virtually forced into concubinage.

[1] The amount varies according to the district, and is sometimes fixed by law, which may remain a dead letter. Sometimes, missionaries manage to elicit a general agreement on a basic figure, which, for the most part, depends on the economic state of the country and may be 20,000 to 100,000 French francs in poor parts like the Middle Congo, 800,000 to 1,000,000 and more in rich districts like the South Cameroons.

The Church does not condemn all desire to grow rich and powerful, but cannot accept polygamy as a means. It has, therefore, to correct the ideas current, and ceaselessly uphold the natural and divine essentials of marriage, urging them on the faithful. In so doing, it strikes at the base of the existing life of the family and society, and the reaction provoked may be violent. The following is an example of the sort. In the summer of 1955, a few local chiefs surrounded the Catholic mission in a village of the central Cameroons, prevented the people from going to Mass, and threatened the missionary with violent measures if he did not change his way of acting. They charged him with implanting outrageous ideas in the minds of young women, urging them to marry only Christians, to refuse to enter a polygamous household, and to become nuns if they had the vocation. This was to deprive the heads of village or family of monetary gain or sensual gratification, and they had no intention of allowing it. Intervention from various quarters put an end to open hostility, but it left the feeling of resentment.

Difficulties equally grave, though not so directly apparent, arise from the traditional form of the family. The origin of these types is still obscure and a matter of dispute. Religious beliefs, historical circumstances, economic needs, have all played a part in it. The scarcity of food, in particular, leads to the dispersion of families over vast areas, and so to the extension of the bonds of consanguinity. In richer lands, it is possible for very large families, comprising several generations, to live together. It is certainly the case in Asia and Africa, as formerly in Europe,[1] that the 'great family' is the prevalent type, one based on descent—paternal or maternal—rather than on the marriage bond.

In Africa to-day, for example,

marriage, while it brings a girl of the clan into another family, does not remove her, juridically, from her original clan; she continues to belong to it. It might almost be said that she is only *lent* to her husband's family for the work of procreation. Nor, in the case of matriarchal clans, does the husband become completely incorporated into his wife's clan; he has no right over his children, who belong to the clan of their mother.

Whether she is a member of a patrilinear or a matrilinear tribe, the African girl grows up with the idea of belonging completely to her own clan. After marriage, she often goes back to it; she knows she will always find protection and support in her difficulties, and a permanent refuge in case of need, should her husband send her away, or should she refuse, after his death, to marry one of his heirs.

Thus, it is not surprising that the African woman remains, primarily the daughter of her 'father' (or, more precisely, of her clan), rather than the mother of her children, *a fortiori* well before being the wife of her husband. For her, the conjugal union only takes third place, and it is not seldom that she refuses to follow her husband when an administrative change, or some other reasonable motive, causes him to leave the country.

[1] Up to quite recent times, the 'family tie' remains very strong in some parts of Europe among peasants in particular. The 'grandfather exercises a quasi-dictatorial power on the rest of the family and over its property, though this is less and less recognized by the law.

Furthermore, when she is recalled to the village for whatever reason by order of her father or of the head of the clan, she obeys without question, leaving without scruple—if not without regret—her husband and children, until she is allowed to go back to them.[1]

In China, where the family is also of the patriarchal type, the conjugal bond seems much stronger, but has a pronounced bias in favour of the wife. Though tradition has come to confine the Chinese wife more and more closely to the home, there

on the contrary, woman has always been the despot of the family. The authority of the mother and the mother-in-law is very well known. Even the wife is always the terror of the husband; no other country in the world can compete with China for the distinction of being the nation of hen-pecked husbands. Certainly, no other country has produced so many stories of hen-pecked husbands. The wife built up her strong position sometimes upon love, sometimes upon beauty or personality, but in most cases upon the fact that she could not be dislodged from her position: she could not be divorced![2]

When several generations live together under the authority of the head of the family, it is his mother or wife who has the power. Hence the saying of Lin Yutang, that a Chinese 'does not marry a wife, but "marries a daughter-in-law", as the idiomatic expression

[1] Marie-André du Sacré-Cœur, *Civilisation en Marche*, Paris, Grasset, pp. 171-172.

[2] Hu Shih, *The Chinese Renaissance*, The Haskell Lectures, 1933 (University of Chicago Press, 1934), pp. 104-105.

goes, and when a son is born, the idiomatic expression is "a grandson has been born" '.[1]

The Church neither has nor could have any objection on principle to these or other types of family life, provided that they observe the law of monogamy and indissolubility, with which they are not incompatible; but it obviously introduces factors making for profound changes in them. No doubt it insists on the obedience due from the wife to the husband, and from children to parents (Eph. 5: 22-6: 4; Col. 3: 18-21; 1 Pet. 2: 13-17), but this obligation is not unrestricted in scope. The 'great family' holds it self-evident that individuals are strictly subordinate to the interests of the group; its head naturally tends to be an autocrat, and to stifle, rather than encourage personal initiative. The Church, while recognizing that family solidarity calls for sacrifices, and that the heads of families often work with intelligence and success for the happiness of all the members, yet promotes the sense of personal vocation; it teaches its members that the call of God has priority over all else, that the religious vocation involves a breaking away from family obligations, and that the call to the married state is a call to set up a home based on love freely given,[2] and rules out any separation of the

[1] Lin Yutang, *My Country and My People*, (Heinemann, 1936), p. 141.

[2] This does not necessarily imply that the choice of husband or wife is left entirely to the two persons, nor does it preclude all intervention on the part of the parents for the good of the two parties or even for that of the family as a whole. Traditions and mental outlooks vary, but they may be perfectly sound. It is constraint that is ruled out. See the very pertinent accounts of Dr John Wu, *Beyond East and West* (Sheed and Ward, 1951).

partners on the pretext of obedience to the head of the family.

What is less apparent in the beginning, but more revolutionary in the end, is the change of emphasis in what constitutes family unity. Whereas the 'great family' is based primarily on blood-relationship or the maternal relation, and the father or mother has, by tradition, a sacred character, the primary factor, in the Christian view, is the marriage bond; this it is which is consecrated by the sacrament of marriage, and raised to the level of a symbol of the mystical union between Christ and his Church (Eph. 5: 25-32); henceforth from it the other bonds derive their strength, which, none the less, is somewhat impaired.

Thus the strictly religious element in family life is seen clearly. The family is never a purely secular institution, except in the secularized Western societies; it rests on beliefs from which it derives its essential strength, and which are expressed in a whole group of various rites, such as the worship of ancestors, or in ceremonies which mark the different stages of life. Ancestor-worship is not necessarily a superstitious practice. In certain circumstances, and when there is no danger of a false construction being placed on it, the Church may authorize its members to take part in it; in other circumstances, she forbids it. Similarly, rites of initiation, of marriage and of burial, may have a primarily social meaning, as the ability of a young person to fend for himself, the mutual consent of the spouses and the alliance between families. Funerals, since they signify the passage to the next world, are necessarily more stamped by the traditional beliefs; but the other rites nearly always include invocations of divinities and gestures expressing the role attributed to them. For these, prayers to God or the saints must be substituted; that has been done, for instance, in the case of the Chinese marriage customs, of course only in Christian circles. The deciding factor in settling the Christian attitude to a particular ceremony is the meaning generally given to it by public opinion; if it is viewed as a social act, no problem arises; but if it is understood to be a religious act expressing non-Christian beliefs, it is impossible for a Christian to take part in it, until those beliefs have been developed and purified.

The latter has been most often the case, up till quite recent times, precisely because the cultures of Asia and Africa were so deeply impregnated with the 'sacred'; and so Christians were faced with the duty, often a very hard one, of breaking away from traditions held by their families as imperative. They were in consequence liable to be looked upon as traitors and as impious. That is no new accusation; it is the one levelled against the early Christians. The danger is that it may not only induce in the convert himself a feeling of shame, but that his relations too may feel themselves dishonoured. In these countries, public opinion could easily view Christian marriage, lacking the ancestral forms, in the same light as Europeans look on 'free love'. What is even more serious is that the vengeance of their divinities may strike, not only those guilty of the 'sacrilege', but the whole family of whom a member has turned aside from the right way.

Owing to a marriage or to the neglect of some ceremony which for a Christian is incompatible with the faith he professed, his family feels hanging over it a threat which agitates it and may lead it to take violent measures. Legal difficulties, too, may arise, if the law, whether written or customary, holds invalid acts performed without the traditional religious forms. The right of inheritance may thus be questioned, or access to certain positions may be withheld.

To missionaries falls the task of resolving cases of conscience fraught with hardship for their converts; they have to strengthen them against the temptation to return to an easier way of life, to keep them from sinking into a state of discouragement when they feel themselves ostracized. They must also concern themselves with the sudden impact of their procedure—even though wholly supernatural and taken with due prudence—on the life of the family. They know that it is not just a question for them to set up order in place of disorder. There were already in existence sound elements of life, and they are not to be suppressed, but rather embodied in new institutions, and animated by the Christian spirit; this requires great care, and there is danger in postponing the effort. It is not enough to state what is of obligation, what is allowed and what forbidden; men have to be trained to live accordingly.

In this consists the great value of Catholic educational establishments and after-school activities. These, as indeed in Europe, cannot be restricted to implanting secular knowledge, but have to form Christians in the fullest sense of the word. Since they also reach a large non-Christian public, they extend correspondingly the Church's sphere of influence. Even when respect for other convictions and observance of the proper stages oblige the missionary to limit himself strictly to secular subjects, he should set himself to form the character and educate the judgment. The human culture he works to promote is closely bound up with Christian ideals, and aims at directing men towards them; it involves a conflict with the evil tendencies which the native cultural tradition may perhaps promote.

Moreover, this work of education brings with it new problems, arising from its western character. Missionaries have, in fact, not been negligent in 'adapting' themselves. Thus, in the Belgian Congo, they have adopted the African languages for their teaching, and worked out curricula which are not modelled on those of Europe, but correspond to local needs.[1] Elsewhere, they have often made greater use of European languages, and followed more closely the usual syllabus, but this is always because it was thought useful to the people themselves, and not through any wish to westernize them. It is clear, for example, that China, at the beginning of the twentieth century, gave up, of its own accord, its traditional mode of education, to create a new system strongly inspired by Anglo-Saxon methods. India or

[1] This applies to the first stages; subsequently other needs have to be met.

Indonesia had no say in the educational revolution brought about by England or Holland, but, when they began to regain their independence or had already obtained it, they had no idea of calling in question these new types of education. When they consider reforms, they aim at giving more scope to their own cultural inheritance, not at forgoing the benefits of a wide initiation into western culture. The integration we spoke about is in course of accomplishment.

The real problem lies elsewhere, in the actual repercussion of the ideas introduced by western education, with its sense of scientific exactitude and material progress, its cult of freedom and its impatience with traditional discipline. New horizons open out before the mind, by reason of the prevailing atmosphere of the schools and the books made accessible by the education given. In consequence, ways of life established by custom or imposed by economic necessity may come henceforth to seem repugnant. The problem is, perhaps, particularly acute in much of Africa. There the young people, on leaving school, have little inclination to return to the life of the bush. In the villages, they would find themselves again under the dominance of the 'elders', and deprived of the cinema and other resources; they are tempted by the towns, even though they may have to live the miserable life of the unemployed. At the same time, it is found that fathers are disinclined to send their daughters to school; it would be time wasted from work in the fields, but, above all, they would return with the fixed intention of exercising their own choice in marriage, and of insisting that their husbands treat them on a footing of equality. These are human problems, admittedly, but they are disturbing to the conscience, and are a threat to the balance of society. The missionary, if he does not take them into account and attempt some solution, will be producing a crop of rootless persons, who would soon grow discontented and embittered, and blame their misfortunes on the Church. The work of education, then, is incomplete and defective, so long as it envisages only the school-period; it has to be concerned with adapting the pupils to the actual life they will have to live, and helping them to discover the resources to sustain and improve it. In addition, it must act, through influencing parents, to alter the surroundings the children will return to when their studies are over, so as to create an atmosphere favourable to the development of their lives as human beings and Christians. In short, education has to be thought out as an organ of the whole life of society.

The Church and Social Life

The new ideas on family life and education brought in by the Church react strongly on the whole culture. They affect the process of acculturation at that very point where the younger generation, of its own accord, takes up and assimilates its ancestral traditions, but it may also transform them more or less radically.

At the same time, as we have already seen, the Church's concern to make it possible for its members to live a fully Christian life leads it to intervene in all the aspects of social life. If it is to direct the whole people towards a life in full accord with the moral law, it has to remove the obstacles in the way of their progress to Christ.

The Church, then, will condemn unnatural customs such as slavery, the killing of infants and prisoners of war, the suicide of widows, the absolute segregation of castes. In regard to the problems arising from urbanization and industrialization, it has to set its face against communism and the abuses of capitalism, against shanty-towns and sweated labour, against arrogant and aggressive race-theories.

In its courteous attitude to all with whom it comes in contact, the Church, in the persons of its members, will set a firm example of the respect due to human dignity. It will labour constantly to restore a true sense of values, and so to foster and encourage really human living conditions. For the want of freedom in its true sense, and excessive poverty, especially when they derive from the way things are organized, hinder both normal human development and the progress of the Christian life.

In regard to social institutions that are either evil or clearly imperfect, the Church's primary and imperative duty is to declare the moral law. Even so, charity obliges it to do so in a reasonable manner and to choose the right moment, and also to observe proper order in the carrying out of its various tasks. It is well known that institutions are not capable of being transformed overnight, and that they are important less for what they are than for the spirit they manifest. Even when imperfect, as everything human is bound to be, they provide an indispensable framework of living; they are not to be abolished until they can be replaced, and undue haste may result in great harm being done. We have only to consider the dramatic consequences of the sudden suppression of slavery in the French colonies under Louis-Philippe. In a few months the colonists found themselves without any workers. Once liberated, the natives had no wish to remain under their former masters, of whom they had only unpleasant memories; yet, accustomed as they were to have food and lodging provided, they could not at once grasp the need for earning their living. The whole community, in fact, was threatened with disaster, which would have benefited no one at all. In itself, the decree of liberation was both generous and just, but it would have been better for everyone if the process had been made more gradual.

This explains why it is that the Church adapts itself, at any rate provisionally, to institutions that are imperfect, or even evil. As we have seen, the early Church refrained from starting a movement against slavery. In seventeenth-century India, and even in our own day, it has not urged the abolition of the caste system, but agrees to tolerate, even in churches, the separation imposed by custom. In the United States, it accepts the provision of separate priests for the whites and for the coloured. In consequence, it has been blamed for belying its vocation. Gandhi, among others, strongly condemned its toleration of caste prejudice.

This, however, is due to a misunderstanding of the nature of the Church's vocation, whose specific aim is the conversion of the hearts of men, the propagation of a certain spirit. This is done more by introducing into the lump a leaven so as to raise it, rather than an explosive charge to reduce it to fragments. The Church brings about the realization of what real love of others consists in, and only thereby undermines institutions opposed to this. It is a love which impels the individual to put himself at the service of all, and so destroys egoism, the source of all enmity. Though uncompromising in regard to evil systems, it is lenient to individual persons, whose responsibility is lessened by their deep-rooted prejudices; so it guards against ill-considered haste, which would only retard progress, and perhaps introduce chaos instead of order and peace.

It is none the less true that the Church, acting through its members, whether native or foreign to the place, aims at developing institutions productive of good, and also at the improvement and reform of those that are defective. Thus, Mother Javouhey founded the celebrated agricultural settlement of Mana (Guiana) to prepare slaves for emancipation. So too, at the end of the nineteenth century, Father Lievens, stirred by the wretched condition of the peasants of Chota Nagpur, cruelly exploited by their zamindars, embarked on a study of the laws, both written and customary, which governed them, became their legal adviser, and founded co-operatives to protect their interests, improve their methods of work, and raise their material level. In a different setting, missionaries introduced syndicalism into Madagascar and elsewhere in Africa.

In his promotion of social welfare, the missionary, while actuated by his Christian spirit, draws on his own cultural experience. In dealing with problems of a like nature, his fellow-countrymen have also worked out solutions in harmony with their own interests and outlook. These have turned out more or less successful, effective or otherwise, and their forms vary according to the difference in western peoples from one another. These solutions may be penetrated with the Christian spirit, or capable of receiving it, or they may be conceived in a frankly materialist way. The institutions therefore, with which the missionary is familiar cannot be looked on as providing a ready-made solution; they call for reflection, comparison, and transposition. He should gather all the information he can, and use his imagination so as to apply only what is best in all the varied experience of the West, and to adapt it to the character of the people concerned.

All this is really the province of lay people; but it may fall to the missionary, in their absence, to take the initiative, and to supply what is needed for the time being. In so doing, he is prompted by the urgency of the need, but he must never forget that he has to train the laity to take over their own responsibilities. This is the real function of lay missionaries; that of the priest is to foster the Christian life in all who come to him, teaching them its essential principles, from which they should draw the practical consequences in every aspect of social life.

The most delicate problems are those which arise from the embodiment of religious elements in social conduct. Just as a group of young Catholics forge certain spiritual links of their own by associating in common prayer, so in all countries of the world, associations of men, women, youths of both sexes, are bound together by participation in certain ceremonies. In the country of Bamileke in the Cameroons, the chiefs, in the summer of 1955, tried to revive certain customs which had more or less lapsed. Among other things, they tried to renew the gatherings of young people. A number of African priests, sent by the bishop of the place, had to enjoin the Christians not to take part in these, unless the fetishist rites, traditionally of obligation, were left out. The native mind, in fact, cannot conceive the possibility of taking part in an act of religion without sharing the beliefs it expresses.

Though the Church does not, in all cases, forbid attendance at non-Catholic religious ceremonies, it has always warned its members against any conduct that would give an impression of indifferentism. It recognizes and respects the genuine religious intention present in the minds of men of very various beliefs, but it is also bound to testify, on every occasion, that it acknowledges as alone true, in the full sense, the revelation brought by Christ and entrusted by him to his Church. The combination of firmness and tolerance, both equally necessary, though on different levels, undoubtedly puts the Church in a difficult position, and its members will not find it easy to avoid exaggeration of one or the other.

The right line of conduct to be followed is particularly difficult to discern when it is a question of beliefs that are absolutely fundamental. According to specialists in the ethnography of the coloured African races, the land is generally held by them to be something divine, and between it and man are set up relations in which divine and human elements are mingled; these are expressed in rites of consecration, at the time of the foundation of villages, and in the system of agricultural work through the seasons. Hence comes the reservation of the work of reclamation to men and that of sowing to women, as we have seen. Besides the land which produces it, food also has a sacred character.

Eating is not only a physical, but also a sacred act. What one eats, how one eats, with whom one eats, are factors that give rise to feelings at a very deep level, sentiments that are not only the most firmly embedded in the individual, but the most far-reaching in their social influence. There is a kind of modesty in the fashion of eating as there is a sexual modesty, and they are constantly associated, whether they are observed for themselves, as in the prohibition of men and women eating together, or as serving to express a subtle distinction of worth. One does not eat red turtle-dove, just as one does not sleep with a woman of a particular clan.[1]

[1] Ch. and M. Le Coeur, *Initiation à l'hygiène et à la morale de l'alimentation chez les Djerma et les Peul de Niamey*, I.F.A.N., VIII, 1946. Different customs, but inspired by the same ideas, are to be found in all the negro communities of Africa.

A religious bond joins those who share the same meal.

This may enable us to understand better what St Paul meant when he wrote: 'In eating, in drinking, in all that you do, do everything as for God's glory' (1 Cor. 10: 31). Quite apart from the special myths of non-Christian religions, and even prior to any divine revelation, it is incumbent on man to recognize the earth and the food it produces as gifts of God. The Church, in restoring this attitude to its original purity of expressing the worship of God in his Providence, does not destroy tradition, but fulfils it.

None the less, mythical beliefs, more or less false, are in fact conjoined with this true religious attitude, and may in some way distort it. It is never easy to find the practical means of correcting it, without destroying it. It is appropriate to reflect on the decisions of the 'Council' of Jerusalem (Acts 15: 28-29), and on St Paul's teachings on the use of things sacrificed to idols (Rom. 14: 13-23; 1 Cor. 8-10). The law of Moses laid down for the Jews certain rules in regard to food, which did not apply to Gentile Christians, but, in order not to scandalize their Jewish brethren, the Gentiles had, for the time being, to keep the same rules, at least in part. By the customs of Greece and Rome, slaughtered animals were offered to the gods before being put up for sale. Christians, knowing that these gods were vain idols, could without scruple buy the meat and use it for food, but if someone, whether Christian or not, drew attention to its 'sacred' character, and held the act of eating it to be a sharing in the idolatrous worship, the Christian would have to abstain from it to avoid giving scandal. 'I am free to what I will; yes, but not everything can be done without harm. I am free to what I will, but some things disedify' (1 Cor. 10: 22-23); 'here is a soul for which Christ died; it is not for thee to bring it to perdition with the food thou eatest' (Rom. 14: 15). These are wise and flexible rules for a carefully graduated mode of conduct, neither compromising nor rigid.

With a view to detaching social behaviour from erroneous beliefs, the missionary will be tempted to emphasize its purely natural aspect. He may not be altogether wrong in this, since this element is present, but it would certainly be a mistake to adopt this solution, the easiest way out of the difficulty. The liberty St Paul claims in regard to all things is the 'freedom of God's sons', who await all from God their Father. The apostle keeps within a world that is sacred, and his view is the truly profound one. What is needed, then, is not to 'secularize' ordinary life, but to assist the various peoples to distinguish the religious inspiration by which they were led from the beliefs which expressed it, to bring them to realize that they were already on the way to the one, true God, who is the fulfilment of all their hopes. In this way, there is no danger of causing the disappearance of that sense of the sacred which divine Providence has so strongly stamped on the Asiatic and African mind.

Yet it is still the case that this work will not be achieved without a dissociation, fraught with danger, between the life of the peoples and their traditional beliefs. There is a sense in which peoples, like individuals, have to go through death to attain the Life. This Life comes, not from the earth, or from anything earthly, but from God alone. 'Believe me when I tell thee this; a man cannot see the kingdom of God without being born anew' (Jn. 3: 3).

This irruption of the Life causes a cleavage in the temporal life. The unity of the people is imperilled. It was not just due to chance or political expediency that the principle of *cujus regio, ejus religio*, came to be accepted at the time of the Reformation. However unsound it may be as ruling out freedom of conscience, it does express the strong conviction that religious unity is the most powerful factor making for the unity of a people. Those who have experienced it will forgo it voluntarily. They may admit a multitude of sects and religious groups, provided that these look to the religious tradition of the people as their centre; but they react, as to a mortal threat, against the preaching of a religion which is fundamentally opposed to received ideas.

However charitable and enlightened the conduct of the missionary may be, he cannot spare a non-Christian culture a rupture with its past that imperils its very foundations. Between the old and the new order, there is inevitably a most dangerous period of instability.

The Church and Political Life

Social life reaches its natural fulfilment only within

a political community; for the pursuit of the common good necessitates an authority to direct it, to prescribe the rights and duties of each person, and to co-ordinate their actions in view of a single end. The political community is perfect in its order, that is, it is the most highly wrought type of human society as such; but since this latter is simply the natural stage where personal freedom acts and develops, the State is not an absolute end in itself. It exists for the sake of the person, whose temporal good it has to ensure, but in view of his spiritual development.

The attitude of the Church to the State may perhaps seem paradoxical. On the one hand, it teaches the strict duty of obedience to constituted authority in all that has to do with the affairs of the nation, provided there is no evident sin involved. This submission goes so far that Christians are forbidden to rebel even when persecuted solely on account of their religion. On the other hand, the Church, in virtue of its spiritual sovereignty, claims an absolute right to complete liberty, in preaching, converting, public worship, the setting up of its characteristic institutions, the choice of its rulers, and the exercise of its governing authority. In addition, it enjoins on the civil authority respect for the moral law, and holds it a duty binding on governments to assist its apostolic work, even though it may prefer to dispense with such support so as to preserve the disinterestedness of its mission. Thus, the Church treats with the State as one power with another, though each has authority in its own particular sphere.

To political rulers, even Christian ones, the Church appears as a doubtful ally, ready to support them, but only up to a certain point, ready also to oppose them, but within certain limits. For instance, in the present nationalistic ferment, it is clear that the Church must be opposed to the colonizing States, since it teaches that political liberty is an inalienable natural right, even if its full realization may come about only by degrees. At the same time, it is in opposition to the new nations, since it teaches the injustice of infringing the lawful interests in their lands acquired by their former rulers, and that 'racialism in reverse' is no less to be condemned than the other sort.[1]

In these, as in other cases, the Church takes its stand on principle, by reason of its being entrusted with the conscience of peoples. The application of principles is not its direct concern; it may suggest one or another type of concrete solution to the problems at hand, but never mobilizes its members in a political action of which it takes over the direction. Temporal intervention of that sort would be contrary to its nature. But its members, as both Christians and members of the community, have the duty to translate that spirit into action, and, in so doing, to further the common good. They must, in consequence, perceive the practical conclusions

---

[1] The Africans, perhaps more than others, have suffered and still suffer from racialism, so obviously prevalent among the whites, many of whom have come to realize that their resentment is tending to crystallize in a negro racialism, out of hostility. The latter is sometimes called 'racialism in reverse' because it is not so much a spontaneous attitude, as a reaction to the conduct of the whites.

to be drawn from the principles laid down, and use the lawful means at their disposal to effect them.

It is not always easy, in the concrete instance, to distinguish between the just and the unjust, the desirable and the possible, nor to work out a solution which respects the rights of all. So it is perfectly natural for Christians to uphold opposing policies. In no case, however, do they act as representatives of the Church, although it is their faith that requires them to foster the civic virtues, and to take part in temporal activities in the service of the national and human communities. They submit to the government when it issues orders within the scope of its lawful powers; they have equally the right and the duty to check or prevent its action, by lawful means, when it seems to them contrary to the rights of their fellow-citizens or of other peoples.

Though the acts of the Church and those of Christians are quite distinct, there is a constant tendency to confuse them, especially when they are looked at from the outside. This confusion naturally arises from the fact that the Church's agents are the hierarchy and the clergy, who are human beings and citizens of a country with whose fortunes they are intimately concerned; being only fallible, they may easily come to confuse their supernatural mission with a temporal line of action. On this account, and also owing to the tendency of politicians to see everything in terms of politics,[1] they

---

[1] Simply through professional bias; not necessarily on account of ignorance, or wilful misunderstanding, of the Church's transcendence.

often look on the Church as a rival power, on the same level as the State.

It is, of course, true that Christians are a force in politics, strong in proportion to their numbers, their abilities, their solidarity, and also their international connections. It is equally obvious that they are profoundly influenced by the Church. From this, it is but a step to conclude to the presence of political aims behind the work of evangelization, or to regard as mere chicanery the assertion of a distinction between the Church and Christians, and this step is only too often taken. It is always difficult for the Church to bring home to people that it is not 'of the world', although sent 'into the world' to restore it to God, the Trinity.

The failure to understand the mystery of the Church has weighed heavily on its historical development. Everywhere, and at every period, governments have tried to make use of the Church to further their temporal aims, or have attempted to prevent its establishment through fear of it bringing in its wake a dangerous political influence.

Without denying the part played by grace, and the powerful witness of the martyrs, we may yet see, in the changed attitude of the Roman Empire, under Constantine, in favour of the Church, an expression of political astuteness; since the State could not destroy this restless and vigorous 'sect', it had to neutralize it or, even better, put it to good use by incorporating it in the social framework, and securing its support by the granting of favours. Constantine himself and his successors, whether deliberately or not, tried to transform the Church into a political force devoted to their interests; and this gave rise to frequent conflicts, for the Church, even if its individual rulers made unfortunate concessions, could never renounce its calling. In spite of all difficulties, a lasting agreement was reached between the Church and the Empire; and this had certain repercussions on missionary activity outside its frontiers. The most characteristic cases are those of Persia and Armenia. Persia, a powerful kingdom, waged war continuously, and often with success, against the Empire. As soon as Rome and the Church reached agreement, the Christians of Persia fell under suspicion and were persecuted, and their progress was halted. However much they protested their loyalty, they were deemed traitors to their sovereign. Armenia, caught between Rome and Persia, was in an unpleasant situation. It was anxious to preserve, if not independence, at least its own traditions. When Persia gained the ascendancy, the Armenians went over to Christianity, partly, but not solely, to ensure the support of Rome; when Rome became the stronger, they embraced heresy, partly to emphasize their independence.

In the sixteenth century, the rulers who shared Vietnam between them, one after the other invited missionaries into their territory, and favoured the growth of Christianity in the hope of obtaining European support against their neighbours, or of enjoying commercial advantages; when their rivals were backed by western powers, they turned against the Church. Japan, for its part, was afraid that missionaries would be the fore-runners of a Spanish invasion; while Siam and China welcomed those sent by Louis XIV.

The whole history of the Church bears witness to the influence of political factors, from one epoch to another, on the course of its development; but to consider them as the sole decisive ones, or even as the most important, would be a grievous error. Their specific effect is to facilitate or impede the contact of the Church with the people, in arousing in them favourable or hostile prejudices. If it be the case that the political climate is favourable, the Church takes advantage from the fact, but its essential task still remains, for to bring forth men to the life of Christ is exclusively the work of the Church and the Holy Ghost, and no other agency can discharge it. If the political climate imposes a barrier, the Church does not admit defeat. It uses all available means to reach the people opposed to it, and to bring the Gospel to them. It has succeeded, both at its first coming and frequently afterwards, in founding vigorous communities in the face of constant persecution. There is only one decisive obstacle to missionary action, and that is the sinfulness of man and his refusal to admit the light.

Still, political factors, like other human agencies, may give rise to secondary hindrances, which missionary action has to take into account. Here the basic diffi-culty lies in the danger of confusing politics and religion, a danger that threatens, not only the authorities of a country, but the missionaries themselves. Viewed, though wrongly, in purely political terms, missionary action seems to endanger the country, both because it is carried on by foreigners, and because it implants ideas that are new and unfamiliar. Consequently, it seems to involve the twofold danger of foreign interference in politics, and cultural and social upheaval.

The Gospel, both of its own nature and by reason of its messengers, impinges sharply on family and social life. The ruling powers fear to see their authority weakened, for Christian teaching severs its connection with the religious sphere where it was formerly exercised, and with the traditional beliefs on which it was based. They may also fear to see the unity of the country impaired, since it would no longer be held together by a single faith and identical habits. Christians, in fact, hold aloof from certain points of the common tradition, and associate themselves besides with a vast international society, whose source and centre lie outside their own country, and whose aims are not so easy to discern.

Much uneasiness will be avoided if the missionary shows that he respects the authorities of the country, is not too critical of its ancestral customs, and takes part in the culture of his adopted country as far as it is not incompatible with the Christian spirit. None the less, the missionary, by reason of his birth, his culture, and the contact he maintains with his native country,[1]

---

[1] The missionary cannot break off all contact with his native country. He is dependent on it for financial support, for fellow-workers and persons to succeed him, not to mention the need for communication with his ecclesiastical superiors, and the indispensable moral support he derives from his friends and his brethren.

is always a foreigner, and, therefore, his acts are bound to cause constant misgiving.

Whatever his wishes in the matter, his conduct is bound to interest his own country, for from it he draws most of his resources.[1] The State, too, however desirous to serve the Church, will be tempted to use the opportunity for its own advantage. Francis I obtained from the Sublime Porte a kind of protectorate over the Christians of the Near East, and, thanks to that, France has been able, through the centuries, to be of the greatest assistance to them; yet the main object was to secure the alliance of the Turks against the Holy Roman Empire. Even more were the 'laic' governments of France, at the beginning of the twentieth century, concerned with the work of the missions because they counted on drawing political advantages from it; none the less, they were most effective in securing for the missionaries their necessary freedom of action.[2]

Whatever benefits may accrue from political intervention on these lines, it always involves a formidable danger. The State is seldom disinterested in its action,

[1] For all sorts of reasons, the State may be led to give direct aid to the work of the missions. Even voluntary organizations in support of the missions are dependent on the good-will of the State, which can either permit or forbid sending men and money to foreign parts.

[2] We are not concerned here to draw up a balance-sheet of political intervention in the mission-field. We will, however, observe that, contrary to prevalent opinion, such intervention was never due to reasons exclusively or even primarily of a missionary character. It was invariably necessitated by political motives, and was clearly directed to political ends, even though the government, in some cases, went on to secure certain advantages for the missionaries.

and naturally looks for some return for its services, using these to bring pressure on the missionary so that he may further its aims, or else, unknown to him, exacting from the country where he works some return for his labours. The missionary, too, from a natural motive of patriotism, may be led to use his position to serve his own country. But even the appearance of collusion between the Church's work in the missions and the political designs of the State is most injurious to the apostolate, not only for the reasons, so obvious and compelling, peculiar to the circumstances of the present, but also because the confusion it inevitably involves may completely hide from view the supernatural character of the Church.

The fundamental law binding on the missionary is none other than God's command to Abraham: 'Leave thy country behind thee' (Gen. 12: 1). He leaves for the country God has shown him, to further the spiritual good of his adopted country, but also, as a consequence of this, its temporal good. He has, therefore, to refuse absolutely to let his hands be tied, and must assert, in regard to his native country, his complete freedom in the discharge of his mission. He may not hesitate to incur the dissatisfaction of his own countrymen and run the risk of losing their support, rather than sully his work by any colour of political action to their advantage.

His very devotion to his adopted people may bring them to hold his native country in high regard; but this is a consequence that should not be consciously desired or sought. The missionary is sent by God for the spread of his kingdom, and so is called to be perfectly disinterested, both as regards his country and his own personal interests.

At the same time, he himself and the Church he brings into being have the urgent duty to take part in the life of the country, where the kingdom of Christ is to be established. The Church of China, of the Congo, or anywhere else, has to take its share in the responsibilities of the country, to make its own the sufferings and joys of the people, to lend its support to whatever makes for human betterment, and to be subject to the laws of the country, except when they contravene its mission. It instils patriotism into its members, not to gain sympathy for itself, but because that is part of the ideal it aims at. Obedience to authority, taught as obligatory on Christians, is not merely passive and inert, but involves active participation in the common effort. Notwithstanding his alien origin, the missionary is bound by loyalty to his adopted country, but he must be extremely careful that nothing may sully the purity of his actions.

Any direct political action, in fact, is dangerous for a local Church, for it is bound to cause confusion between missionary work and work for a temporal end. It is no more normal for the clergy, native or foreign, of a missionary country to enter the political arena than it is for those in countries where Christianity is of long standing. It may not always be forbidden for a priest to take part in politics, but it only happens in exceptional cases, and by the express approval of his bishop.

It is, however, indispensable to form the civic con-science of Christians. At first, they may seem wholly absorbed by the discovery of the supernatural world opened out before them; they may feel themselves ineffectual, on account of their small number, or dis-couraged by the distrust felt for them. This may easily give rise to a kind of political apathy, which may reinforce the prejudice of their countrymen against the Church. What is necessary is to arouse the Christians to a sense of their national and social responsibilities, to accustom them to reflect on the problems that arise, to aid them to work out their solutions, and to bring them to realize that they have to work towards the reign, in their country, of peace, justice and charity.

The Church itself may have to take a definite line in public, when the vital interests of the nation are involved. Thus, the apostolic delegate to China, and all the bishops of the country, denounced in concert the Japanese aggression of 1937, and called all Christians to their duties as patriots. In the same way, the South African bishops protested strongly against the policy of *apartheid* rampant, and those of Madagascar and French Africa proclaimed unequivocally the right of their people to independence.

As its vocation demands, the Church, on these and similar occasions, confines itself to the sphere of prin-ciples; it is no part of its mission to state the precise means by which, in practice, they are to be applied. As guardian of both social and individual morality, it appeals to the conscience and good will of all to let social life be brought ever more completely in accord with the moral law, and, as soon as possible, be guided by the supernatural light of Christ. But it is for men, each in his own sphere, to work out ways of living that will foster their ascent to God.

In the present crisis of the world, where we see intermingled, in every country and race of mankind, so much unselfish devotion and egoistic striving, so many generous aspirations and fantastic imaginings, so much narrowness of view and resentful feeling, there is nothing more urgent, however impolitic it may be, even for man's temporal salvation, than to blazon abroad Christ's call to charity, that real charity poured out by the Spirit, which alone is capable of passing beyond justice in order to uproot the injustice and resentment in the hearts of men.

Outlook for the Future

The network of human relations is bound to be more or less disturbed by the action of the Church; for it penetrates deeply into the temporal order to cure its ills and raise it to a higher plane, and, in so doing, the Church is permanently liable to misunderstanding.

Quite apart from any religious motives, everyone is concerned with social progress in its various forms, and has his own special responsibility and part to play in its promotion. When the Church sets about restoring the solid foundations on which all progress depends, or collaborates in the works of men, its action appears no different specifically from that of any other organization. When the African or Asiatic sees the arrival from Europe of administrators, engineers, doctors, teachers, traders, and missionaries too, how can he be expected to distinguish the latter from all the others? They all of them engage in building, or cultivation, they open schools, hospitals, dispensaries, workshops, and so on.

The missionary brings along with him both supernatural and natural gifts to the country, but they differ completely in their nature. From those of the natural order, everyone may take what pleases him, but the supernatural ones are of absolute necessity to each, even though he has the power to refuse them. The people run the risk of confusing the two kinds. They may refuse grace, because the culture in which it is presented does not appeal to them; but they may accept it simply as something of no particular importance that goes with the temporal goods they really want.

Yet temporal action, kept in its right place, is good; for it provides the Church with numerous opportunities for contact and evangelization. By its means, the Church shows that her charity is genuinely human, because truly divine. It is charity that enjoins her to make known to the peoples of the earth the sole principles of real life. It is charity, too, which impels her to educate her members to lead a fully Christian life, and, to that end, not only to instruct them by word, but to draw them by the example of those of her members whose formation is already complete. Hence, Pius XII makes it a special duty of bishops to found those ' associations and institutions, based on social and economic ties, that are required by the circumstances and the character of the people entrusted to them' (Pius XII, *Evangelii Praecones*). The Church has no design of taking over the direction of temporal matters, or of recommending a particular social or economic system; its mission is only to ensure everywhere the presence of the Christian leaven that may permeate the whole lump.

The missionary who is called upon to deal with temporal matters must bear in mind that these are normally the province of the laity, and that he has to organize them with a view to his own replacement by Christians who are 'competent, of recognized integrity and prudence, to take over these enterprises and develop them' (Pius XII, *Evangelii Praecones*). His function is to make clear what religion demands; he is the conscience, both of the faithful and of the whole people. Ever sensible of his supernatural mission, which has absolute priority, he will make it his chief aim to express in visible form the spirit which animates him in all that he does.

It may be that he will be often discouraged by the way his efforts are received. When Our Lord healed the man born blind (Jn. 9), the bystanders were struck with amazement at such an unheard-of miracle; but, since it happened on a sabbath day, it caused scandal. 'Some of the Pharisees said: This man can be no messenger from God; he does not observe the sabbath. Others asked, How can a man do miracles like this, and be a sinner?'

The missionary, in his turn, will be exposed to malicious interpretations, misconceptions, narrowness, and will experience, too, the joy of seeing men turn to Christ. At one moment, he will be blamed for interfering too much in human affairs, at another, for ignoring them. It is not merely a question of the personal shortcomings, inevitable that they are, of the missionary himself; for, whether from outside or within the Church, the same persons will be found to make diametrically opposed accusations against him on identical points, and will also find much to censure in missionaries who act differently to him.

'To what, then, shall I compare the men of this generation? What are they like? They put me in mind of those children who call out to their companions as they sit in the market-place and say, You would not dance when we piped to you, you would not mourn when we wept to you. When John came, he would neither eat nor drink, and you say, He is possessed. When the Son of Man came, he ate and drank with you, and of him you say, Here is a glutton; he loves wine; he is a friend of publicans and sinners. But wisdom is vindicated by all her children' (Lk. 7: 31-35).

In spite of all the criticism, however, there will also be men who will see the light, as did the man born blind when Our Lord passed by.

In any event, the missionary will remember that it is better to please God rather than men (Gal. 1:10; 1 Thess. 2:4). Consecrated as he is to the service of peoples, he has to further their spiritual good in all the human and social aspects that the fulness of the Christian life implies. He cannot evade this summons. He trusts the charity that is the source of all he does to prove his disinterestedness, that his sole aim is to bring each man to the joy of God.

4

GROWTH OF A LOCAL CHURCH

'THE immediate aim of the missions is to make the light of Christian truth shine before peoples among whom it had never been, and to raise up Christians from among them; but the ultimate end at which they must aim, and which they must have continuously in view, is that the Church should be firmly and definitively set up among the new peoples, with its own hierarchy chosen from among the inhabitants of the country' (Pius XII, *Evangelii Praecones*). In these words, the Pope designates precisely the two stages of missionary work. When the missionaries have proclaimed the word of God, and brought a few persons to the life of grace, there yet remains something more to be done; they have to develop the local Church, which is the universal Church in a particular country, until it reaches maturity.

Evangelize or Humanize

The local Church, in consequence, has to concern itself intimately with the institutions and customs of the people. Its struggle against destitution and injustice, and its active support of cultural progress, enable it to establish contacts and gain the sympathies of the people. Moreover, it is obliged to set right those elements in the native culture that are at variance with the moral law, and to restore the framework of natural morality without which its members could not be led to a full Christian way of living. Finally, since Christian morality is illuminated by Revelation and completely penetrated by grace, and grace takes hold of every side of human life, the Church, by its temporal action, aims not only at creating conditions useful or indispensable to its supernatural action, but also at impregnating the temporal sphere with a specifically Christian spirit.

In consequence, the two aspects, cultural and supernatural, of the missionary's work are not easily distinguishable, when viewed from the outside. Moreover, in the countries to be evangelized, the Church ordinarily finds the religious and the social spheres closely integrated, very slightly differentiated, and each bearing the imprint of the other. Itself a society taking in the whole of man, it easily appears as a competitor on the same plane as the others, an alien force coming in to destroy age-long traditions, and threatening the existence of the nation's personality.

Whether this prejudice is strong or weak, more or less consciously entertained, in the 'people outside', its existence is unquestionable, and gives the missionary much food for thought. A twofold danger confronts him. He may be tempted to explain all the difficulties in his way by certain cultural factors that make the people impervious to his teaching. For example, he may deem it impossible to christianize the people as a whole, or a section of them, so long as they are burdened with this or that institution, whether it is polygamy, or the wage-system, nomadism, or slum-dwelling. He may therefore imagine that all his efforts should be directed to that one point, and that only after their success will he be able to preach the Gospel. Now, it is undoubted that 'inhuman' conditions of life hinder access to the Christian life; but that does not authorize the conclusion that 'humanization' must precede evangelization.

On the other hand, what may strike the missionary as specially significant is the fact that the Church is allied with a particular culture, not essentially indeed, but in so far as he lives and expresses it, as a result of the circumstances of his own upbringing. He may, therefore, come to think that he meets with no response, because the Church, in the concrete, in its missionaries, comes as something 'western' or 'bourgeois'. The aim would then be to restore to the Church its universality untarnished, and this would mean, in fact, its taking on a new individual culture, a new 'humanization'. The conclusion is essentially the same as in the preceding case, though in appearance the reverse. Again, it is a question of 'humanizing' before evangelizing, but now it is the Church that is to be humanized, to be adapted to the people it approaches. In this case, too, it must be recognized that those special features of the Church tend to disguise its real nature, but that is not a sufficient reason for the conclusion that nothing can be done until those features are eliminated.

In both cases, to act accordingly would be to treat the problem on a purely superficial level; it would amount to accepting that the contact of the Church with the peoples is no more than a meeting of cultures, or, at least, that it begins with that, and, in consequence, that it is impossible for grace to be communicated, the word of God to be heard, until the cultural differences have been smoothed over.[1] This is far from the truth.

Christ, who is both our Head and the model we have to follow, has shown us the way. We have already seen that, if he concerns himself with typically human questions, that is because he is truly man and the light he brings illuminates the whole of human life; yet he does not apply himself, in the main, to changing the institutions of society. He does not wait for the abolition of destitution before proclaiming to all the good news of the Gospel, the only message that is absolutely and completely good, that 'God loves men'. Entrance into the Kingdom of God is opened up to all, rich and poor alike. The renewal Christ offers to mankind is an interior one; it acts like the leaven which raises all the lump without ever becoming identical with it. The leaven does not wait for the paste to rise before it gives free rein to its power of expansion, but it itself causes the paste to rise.

Equally clear is the lesson of the early Church, whose action on the question of slavery we have already studied.

[1] On the relation between evangelization and its conditions, see the illuminating point of view of Father Pin, 'Sociologie religieuse et Réflexion théologique', in *Revue de l'Action Populaire*, January 1956, pp. 3-14.

St Paul, fully conscious of his calling to preach the Gospel, and confident in the guidance of the Spirit, was able to declare: 'Being entrusted, then, by God's mercy, with this ministry, we do not play the coward; we renounce all shamefaced concealment, there must be no crooked ways, no falsifying of God's word; it is by making the truth publicly known that we recommend ourselves to the honest judgment of mankind, as in God's sight' (2 Cor. 4: 1-2). 'It would go hard with me indeed if I did not preach the gospel' (1 Cor. 9: 16). It was this obligation of his, inescapable and primary, which led him to live with other men, 'with the Jews . . . like a Jew, to win the Jews . . . with those who are free of the Law like one free of the Law[1] . . . With the scrupulous I behaved myself like one who is scrupulous . . . everything by turns to everybody, to bring everybody salvation' (*Ibid.* 20-22).

The problem before the Church is, in fact, one of visibility, or, perhaps more exactly, of transparence. What is, properly speaking, visible of her, is always one or other of her human aspects, just as Christ himself was for his contemporaries, the 'carpenter's son' (Mt. 13: 55; Mk. 6: 3). It is in the very person of Jesus that the Son of God is revealed; there can be no question of depriving the Incarnate Word of his human features, as if they were nothing but a mask he wore. They are, in fact, an integral part of his person, the sign, the *sacrament* in which he is manifested. But neither are we to stop at the material aspect of the sign; we must

[1] The reference is to those who are not subject to the Mosaic Law.

penetrate to the divine reality which is its origin and which it bears.

That is why Christ asked his apostles: 'Who do you say that I am?' and, when Peter confessed him to be the Christ, the Son of the living God, Christ declared: 'Blessed art thou, Simon son of Jona; it is not flesh and blood, it is my Father in heaven that has revealed this to thee' (Mt. 16: 15-17).

Without grace, it is never possible for man to discern God in the person of Christ, the 'Son of Man'; but the Father works in the hearts of men, opens them to the light, gives them understanding of the works by which the Son of God manifests himself as what he really is. 'If you find that I do not act like the son of my Father, then put no trust in me; but if I do, then let my actions convince you where I cannot; so you will recognize and learn to believe that the Father is in me, and I in him' (Jn. 10: 37-38).

The works to which he refers may be summed up as the giving of himself to man. God's coming among men to share their life, the sovereign Wisdom shedding its light on man, his power placed at the service of men, his own life given to deliver them from death—these are the works that testify to the intervention of God in human history for the benefit of mankind. On this account, men are brought to recognize Christ as their God and Saviour, to see beyond his human appearance the splendour of his divinity.

The Church is nothing else than the *sacrament* in which Christ continues his presence in the world, at all times and in every part. She, too, is manifested to men in human form, in the person of her missionaries, in the local Churches. These rapidly attain visible shape in the countries where they are, at least in a small group of the inhabitants, and from the importance they derive from their union with the universal Church; but, at first, they are perceptible only to the senses, that is to say, they are in danger of appearing as purely human institutions. It is necessary that these human appearances, which are not disguises, but aspects of the Church itself, should become transparent to the supernatural.

That can come about only if grace is active in the souls of the missionaries and their followers to purify continually their actions, and, at the same time, if it opens the hearts of non-Christians to the light, to the understanding of the works wherein the Church, like her Head, shows forth her real nature, which is both divine and human; for Christ has communicated to his Church, not only his love, but his power too. 'The man who has learned to believe in me will be able to do what I do; nay, he will be able to do greater things yet. It is to my Father I am going: and whatever request you make of the Father in my name, I will grant, so that through the Son the Father may be glorified' (Jn. 14: 12-13).

These works are the miracles wrought throughout the generations, and, much more, the evident fruits of the life of the Church in all peoples, the outcome of the heroic charity she stirs up in the hearts of men. Here is a witness of how, on the human countenance of the

Church, her divine features, as it were, become clearly delineated.

> Religion is what the missionaries are concerned with. As their name indicates, they are *sent* for a precise purpose, to be, for the human race, the heralds of God and his revelation. They take on social activities as well, because they see in them a means of bringing men to God, and because they know that injustice is a great evil that outrages the justice of God and injures its victims. If aid to lepers is so esteemed by missionaries, particularly Catholic ones, it is because no other form of service demands a greater spirit of sacrifice; it calls forth the highest idealism and the most complete abnegation. The worlds of politics and journalism can boast few heroes comparable with Father Damien of the leper-colony of Molokai. The Catholic Church, on the other hand, numbers thousands who, like him, have vowed themselves to the service of the lepers. It is well worth our while to study the source of a heroism like that.[1]

Human service of a kind altogether exceptional, that is what stimulates the mind of man to investigate the source whence it springs; but it can be found only if the missionary gives himself out for what he really is, the herald of God. This service, in fact, would take on a false aspect, even to the one who renders it, if he saw it as just a service of the bodily needs of others, of their material, even human, wants, confined to the temporal order. The gift, surpassing human imagination, that God brings to the world, that the missionary is entrusted with to offer to all, is the gift of divine life. It is from

[1] Gandhi, quoted in *Rhythmes du monde*, 1946, no. 2, p. 2.

the Holy Spirit himself, given by God to his Church, that all the works of the missionary spring; to the Spirit and the whole Trinity they must give continual witness. They must ever point to the Spirit, and be the channel communicating him to man.

The Church cannot wait till conditions are favourable before starting the work of evangelization. Peter, threatened by the Sanhedrin, replied boldly: 'God has more right to be obeyed than men' (Acts 5: 29). The apostles, sent to preach the Gospel, allowed no hindrance to deter them. Their successors, at the command of Christ, are ready to go to the ends of the earth, to places where access is barred just as much as to those where they are welcomed, to the hostile and suspicious as well as to the well-disposed and trusting, to people apparently the least likely to receive the gift of God as well as to those the most open to it. Everywhere, it is the message of God, and it alone, that will act as the ferment.

To proclaim Christ's coming to the world and his work of salvation, to gather those called by God and make them grow in the divine life, that is the first task of the Church, to which she is wholly dedicated, and which she cannot evade. But charity urges her, the need for removing obstacles puts her at the service of men; this task, too, is incumbent on her, but it must ever remain a subordinate one.

From whatever standpoint, to suppose that a process of 'humanization' ought to precede the work of preaching the Gospel would be to misunderstand profoundly the true nature of the apostolate, which is essentially a supernatural work. The missionary, as God's instrument, is obliged to put all his talents, whether great or little, at God's service. The actual efficacy of all that he does depends essentially on his docility to the call of God, not on his human talents. The decisive factor is holiness; for what is decisive is the action of God on minds and hearts, and holiness alone, the supreme gift of God, has the privilege of being able to exert an influence on the action of God himself.

It is perfectly clear, too, that the preaching of the Gospel is itself a call to holiness, and that the primary task of the Church is to point out the ways to union with God, to make them available to all, to support them in their endeavour and to remedy their shortcomings, to keep those entrusted to her by God as Christ kept his own (Jn. 17 : 12). The Church, therefore, must organize the life of her members in such a way that they may have access to the source of life. She must make herself visible and permanent enough for the people, and every man of good will, to be able to discover her, recognize her for what she is, give her their adherence, and, by her mediation, become themselves sons of God.

The Christian Family

The family, besides being the natural basis of all human society, is also destined by God to be an integral part of the structure of the Church. For, since it is entrusted with the task of bringing up children to become men in the fullest sense, it has, at the same time, the vocation to make them sons of God, and, in consequence, it is the centre from which the Christian spirit radiates into the whole life of the community.

With regard to the family, as to every other institution of the natural order, the Church's role is not 'creative'; she does not have to bring it into being, in all its parts, out of nothing. She does not aim at altering its traditional social and legal status, except in so far as this deviates from the natural law. What she does do is to exercise on it an action of 're-creation', admitting her members to the sacrament of marriage and leading them on to live it fully; thus, she raises the family to the supernatural level, and gives it, through grace, the power to form children to be true Christians.

The specific function of the missionary is to bring the family to realize the full depth of the love which is spiritual, and so to put physical love in its right place, so that it comes to foster and develop a love that is properly human, that is one where the flesh is subservient to the spirit, and not the contrary. At a much higher level, this human love will come to be made fruitful and to be raised up by the inflowing of divine love. The missionary brings to the family a whole spiritual outlook that goes beyond the keeping of the commandments, and introduces it to a religious life lived as a community, and no longer just individually. The marriage bond, as a symbol of the unity of Christ and his Church, should be lived in the fulness of its mystical significance.

This ideal can be realized in a great many different ways. It does not necessarily require the break-up of the 'great family' in all its forms, though it alters the balance within it, as we have seen. Nor does it demand that the law, written or customary, of a country should admit the full legal and social status that Christian marriage has a right to. In Italy, Christian marriage is, as such, valid in law, and is subject to the Canon law, but there are few countries now which recognize it in the same way; yet this does not make it impossible for the Christian family to exist and to reach its full development. In this way, Christian liberty is emphasized, as well as a fact essential to the growth of the Church, namely, that its foundations can and must be laid even though human institutions have not yet developed to the state which they ought to reach.

Family life, informed by grace, furthers the spiritual life of husband and wife, and its influence naturally spreads into their surroundings. The children will be the first to benefit from it, and it is by no means one of the least concerns of the Church to prepare parents for their function as educators. Normally, it will continue their work in its own schools and other places of instruction, which, therefore, meet the need both of preparing the non-Christian pupils to receive the Gospel message, and of forming the Christians to lead a fully Christian life. There is bound to arise a certain tension between these two objects, but there can be no question of sacrificing one to the other.

The family environment thus 're-created' is a suitable

centre where new converts are welcomed, and so avoid the danger of being totally uprooted. It is the natural nursery for the germination and ripening of apostolic vocations, whether of priests or laity, which the Church needs in order to continue and widen the scope of its activity.

The part of the laity in the mission field is an important one, and Pope Pius XII treats of it at length in the encyclical *Evangelii Praecones*. Frequently in the course of history, the Pope reminds us, priests were preceded in new countries by laypeople who prepared the soil and sowed the seeds of the Christian life. Like the Magi of old, certain men of learning from Korea, struck by the truth of God which they read about in a book of Father Ricci, travelled, in the middle of the seventeenth century, to Pekin to obtain a fuller knowledge of Revelation, and ask for missionaries to be sent to them. It was many years before priests went to teach them in their own country, but, when they arrived, they found a whole Christian community had been gathered and instructed by the travellers on their return. Often, in the course of their investigations, missionaries have come upon fields white with the harvest that only awaited their arrival to reach perfect maturity.

Everywhere, lay missionaries are called to 'exercise a salutary influence, setting up charitable works, spreading the Christian faith in every part, supporting the cause of the Church to their full ability, above all, pointing the way to all men by their personal example' (Pius XII, *Evangelii Praecones*).

They are helpers, often indispensable, in the work that falls to the clergy. Thus, they may become catechists, that is to say they are entrusted with much of the work of leading catechumens to the Church, instructing them in religion, and assuring their perseverance by organizing prayer in common and meetings for the furtherance of their spiritual life. It is no detraction from the heroism and zeal of the missionaries to recognize the immense work done by the catechists. They, trained and supported by the missionaries, may justly claim that the actual development of the Churches of Asia and Africa are, in great measure, due to their efforts.

They have, too, their own specific role, which consists primarily in showing by their own life that Christianity is not just a matter for priests and religious, but can be lived completely in the temporal setting, and brings to it a peace and joy surpassing any human expectation. From this a second aspect is derived, which is to further Christian solutions of temporal problems, and so to work positively toward the transformation of existing institutions by the Christian spirit.

By Baptism and Confirmation, every Christian is called to this apostolate, and he has all sorts of means to exercise it. The life and conduct of Christians create, in the world, a tissue of spiritual influences which draw non-Christians to embrace Christianity and sinners to amendment of life. What is still too often lacking to Christians aware of this vocation of theirs is the practice of meeting together for a more thorough initiation into their responsibilities, and for the extension of their range of action on the whole of social life. That is the function of Catholic Action.

This is how a Christian community comes into being and develops, but only on condition that there is present within it the priesthood, through which the supernatural life is given.

The Clergy

From the earliest times, one of the chief preoccupations of the apostles, whenever the Holy Spirit raised up by their preaching a new Christian community, was to appoint 'elders', priests, with the charge of conveying to others the supernatural life they had received, and to watch over the growth of this life in the local Church. They chose these 'elders' from the district, though the practice was not ruled out of transferring a priest or bishop from one locality to another. The Congregation of Propaganda, from its beginning, insisted on the urgent necessity of forming an indigenous clergy, from which ultimately the local bishops would be chosen. The Popes of modern times, who insist so strongly on the development of a native clergy, refer constantly to the tradition derived from the apostles.

The bishop is not just an administrator. Representing God to man, he is equally the representative of man before God, and so he must be 'chosen from among his fellow-men' (Heb. 5: 11), truly one of them, chosen by God as mediator between them and him. That is the normal law, and a foreigner cannot fulfil it entirely. If the Church is fully entitled, after considering all the circumstances of time and place, to call anyone it pleases to govern a diocese, it only chooses a foreigner for some exceptional reason, or because the local Church is not judged to be yet mature enough.

This question of maturity is a delicate one, and the Holy See is the ultimate judge of it. It is certainly not bound up essentially with the material extension of the local Church, that is with the number of members, or even of priests; but it depends rather on the consciousness of priests of their responsibilities. If they are too much attached to the human prestige accruing to them, or if they fail to understand the thorough detachment required by their priesthood from their family and all human ties, they may well be able to represent their people before God, but they are ill suited to be the true representatives of God to men. All through her history, in every country, the Church has had to struggle against the domination of priests by their families, a domination which is especially pernicious when exerted over bishops, who are then dangerously liable to let temporal interests prevail over their duties.

The Church has no need to despair in the face of human weakness, or to lack confidence that the Spirit will raise men of good will to the height of their vocation, but she has to use supernatural wisdom in choosing bishops as in accepting priests for ordination, both rejecting the unsuitable and fixing the duration of the preliminary stages.

It is, however, also a matter of supernatural wisdom

to take account of practical conditions. It is clear that foreign missionaries will never be sufficient for the evangelization of a country; those who are to replace them must be chosen from the place. The natives are no less able than foreigners to absorb the Christian spirit, enter upon the understanding of the Christian mysteries, preach the Gospel to their people, advance in the way of sanctity. They may be better able than foreigners to gain access to certain quarters closed to others, and to perceive how to reach the hearts of men. Moreover, the supply of foreign missionaries may, for various reasons, dry up, or they may come to be forbidden entry into the country. It is enough to recall the almost total disappearance of missionary personnel following on the French Revolution, the internment of many of its active staff in the late wars, and the difficulties caused by the arousing of national consciousness in Asia and Africa.

No one has ever questioned the necessity of forming, sooner or later, a national clergy in every country where Christianity has taken root, and of entrusting it with all responsibility for the Church of the district. Everywhere immense efforts have been made to attain this end. It was the chief concern of St Francis Xavier, as it was the essential function entrusted to the Vicars Apostolic at the request of Propaganda in the seventeenth century. At times, however, the possibility has seemed doubtful of reaching this result in the near future. The difficulties are, in fact, considerable, for the formation of a local clergy requires the fulfilment of conditions which are not easy to satisfy or to harmonize with each other.

While Benedict XV and Pius XI insisted most strongly on hastening the development of the clergy, they opposed with equal vigour the temptation to admit candidates too readily. It is not just a question, for the missionaries, of enlisting minor auxiliaries, to be kept in a subordinate position, but of raising up pastors and apostles who will take over the Christian destinies of their people.

Candidates therefore must by their temperament and proved trustworthiness show a real prospect that they will persevere in their vocation. They must be given a spiritual and theological training at least equal to that given in the older Christian countries, in fact a more advanced one, for the work before them is formidable and intricate.

As things are at present, the education of the clergy involves learning Latin and scholastic philosophy, for the Church's tradition is expressed in those terms. There is no question of dispensing seminarists from these studies, even if they are foreign to their culture. The pontifical decrees are explicit on this point, for the clergy must be brought into contact with the sources of Christianity. Besides, at a time when Western culture has spread all over the world, and has been eagerly assimilated by the educated everywhere, it is far from strange, indeed it is most desirous, that the clergy should profit from it too, and steep themselves in its noblest element, the Christian tradition. Not that this tradition itself is properly part of a culture, but the latter is an indispensable road, at least provisionally, to its understanding.

In consequence of such a formation, the clergy run the risk of becoming partly divorced from their own culture. The young priests, brought up on the traditional ecclesiastical disciplines, may speak in terms that mean little to their compatriots, whether these are still formed solely by their ancestral traditions, or are already influenced by the prevailing westernizing trend. They must, therefore, still receive a thorough grounding in their own culture; but the simultaneous pursuit of both these ends demands a high degree of courage, industry, and perseverance.

The solution of the difficulty lies in a proper balance and proportion; it requires delicate adjustment and a fairly long period of time. The crucial point lies beyond the problems of instruction; for, above all, there must be developed in the young clergy 'the sanctity demanded by the priestly life, an apostolic spirit and a concern for the salvation of their brethren that will make them ready to give even their lives for the members of their tribes and nations' (Pius XI, *Rerum Ecclesiae*). In missionary, just as in Christian, countries, the priest is foremost a 'man of God', who lives by and for God, and so is, in fact, dedicated to the service of men. If the seminarist, and the priest too, does not see his vocation in this light, he fails to understand its nature, and his ministry will be ineffectual.

Whatever state of development a local Church may

have reached, the primary functions of the clergy, indigenous or foreign, are always and everywhere the same. The Church, like Christ, was sent to save mankind by imparting to it divine charity; but the mode of redemption chosen by Christ is none other than the liturgical sacrifice of the Cross, which gives to God a perfect worship and causes the outpouring of grace to men. Consequently, the offering of the Mass, where the Church unites itself to Christ's offering and becomes a sharer in his grace, is the very centre of its life, and is, *par excellence*, the function of the priest. All the rest of his activities serve as preparation for it and as disposing others to unite themselves to it, or else to gather and communicate its fruits. The Eucharist is the living spring whence the Church draws its nourishment, and to which the faithful must be led that they too may draw on it and satisfy their thirst.

Living Water

To bring the whole world to the source of living water, which is Christ himself, is the task for which the whole missionary Church is responsible, each member playing his appropriate part. The functions to be discharged are of various kinds, but all are necessary, and they are exercised in close dependence on the hierarchy, which not only controls, but also creates, them. For it is a question of a strictly supernatural order of activity, which the priesthood alone has received the power to call into being.

The power of preaching is directly connected with the power of Orders, for the presenting of the faith is far more than a matter of teaching. It aims at the conversion of souls to God, and so at eliciting from those who 'hear' the word a personal act, rich in its effects, in which all their faculties are brought into play, under the influence of the grace that comes down on them to 'recreate' nature. To impart the supernatural life the fulness of sacramental grace is needed. The work can be divided up and allotted to various groups: catechists trained to teach doctrine, the lay apostolate set up with its advantage of being on the same footing as the people to be approached, family education established. These are but ways of participation in the strictly priestly action; they have their own kind of perfection, but not the fulness of the apostolic preaching from which their own effectiveness is derived. This flows from the grace of Orders, and needs no special setting; it matters little whether the missionary preaches in the street or from a pulpit. But he cannot fulfil his ministry unless he makes it his aim to gain for himself the fulness of life, which is charity; his preaching is a giving of himself and of the truth living within him, which is, in fact, his very life. It demands, therefore, from him a constant fidelity in directing his mind and heart to God.

This serious application to holiness of life is itself a form of preaching, in fact the most effective of all, even if the results are not always immediately apparent. It is testified to abundantly by history, as, for instance, by

K

that of the origins of the Church of Malagasy. The missionaries there had their own share of the cross, but the way in which the first inhabitants of the country came to accept the Church, more than a century ago, has left a permanent memory. They had seen the missionaries at prayer, and came to tell them: 'We want to pray with you, to pray like you.' A missionary who was no more than a builder or an administrator would have left out what was, in fact, the essential. He would have failed to grasp the lesson handed down by so many others who, in different places, became deservedly known as 'men of prayer'. Only through his continual contact with God in prayer will the missionary be able to detect God's ways with men and learn to lead others to Christ.

In this question of the ways of God, there is one doubt which besets many minds, namely, that, since Christ called to himself, first of all, the shepherds of Bethlehem, it would seem fitting to preach the Gospel first to the poor alone, to devote the best part of our attention to the disinherited of this world. To this Pope Pius XI gave a decisive answer:

Undoubtedly, the word of God is received with most alacrity by the poor, as are the preachers of the Gospel themselves. Undoubtedly, too, Christ himself declared: 'The spirit of the Lord has sent me out to preach the gospel to the poor' (Lk. 4:18). But we are not to forget the words of St Paul: 'To the wise and to the unwise I am a debtor' (Rom. 1:14). Besides, we know from actual experience that, once the élite of a country is won over to Christianity, the ordinary people easily come to follow their example (*Rerum Ecclesiae*).

The Church has no choice in the matter. Her mission is to proclaim the Gospel to every man, to let the light of grace shine everywhere. No one can be excluded from it, except through his own fault. The élites, social and intellectual, must be evangelized, and the influence they naturally exert will bring in the rest of the people. But the evangelization of the poor is still the special sign of the coming of Christ, who does not weigh human worth in terms of money, knowledge or power, and it exhibits that charity which perceives, in every human being, the person of Christ (Mt. 25: 31-46).

The act of faith which brings the supernatural life to birth implies the desire for Baptism; but the catechumen cannot be admitted to this sacrament, unless the Church, in the person of the priest responsible, judges him ready to receive the life of Christ, and to be incorporated into the Christian community. Baptism, then, is as much a public act of the Church as a personal adhesion to Christ. The responsibility of the Church is all the greater in that, by Baptism and Confirmation—the fulness of Baptism—the convert becomes a witness of the Church before the world. The other sacraments ensure to this beginning of life its constant growth and purification, to the Church fruitfulness and continuance.

The missionary has to take care that his converts realize the value of the sacraments, for their own religious traditions may, in fact, minimize the importance of outward rites. More often, however, though they do not completely ignore the interior life, non-Christian religions put their chief emphasis on a 'ritual purity' that is wholly exterior, and the catechumens may look upon the rites of the Church in the same light. They must be taught that it is not enough to 'receive' the sacraments, but they must also 'live' them, and they must acquire the sense of the spiritual progress they are required to aim at.

Light and strength will be theirs through the theological virtues, whose principal object is to enable God to be perceived, in the life of the Trinity, as true, good, powerful and ready to succour. They include, in addition, secondary objects which take on a special aspect in missionary countries. In the case of faith, these will be the understanding of the Christian mysteries and the solution of the difficulties, both speculative and practical, arising from the former mode of life. Hope envisages an infant Church, still weak, exposed to reverses of many kinds and often the victim of enmity or persecution. Charity sees every man as 'my neighbour', and recognizes that all, whatever their racial origin, are sons of the same Father, called to the same life. In so far as he lives these virtues, the Christian bears witness before the world. By them, the moral virtues are vivified and restored to their fulness of being. Under their influence, institutions become impregnated with a new spirit. They are the source of the apostolic vigour which is exhibited in an outburst of activities of all kinds, and leads to the supreme witness of martyrdom, if that is what God should ask.

The Christian life reaches its normal development in a country only with the appearance of the religious life in all its forms, communities both of men and of women, devoted to contemplation or apostolic work. Although these ways of life are only for those specially called to them, the religious life is a sign to all Christians, and indeed to all mankind, of the eternal in time. It is, in fact, the most perfect realization of detachment from the earth, and that is always necessary to the Christian; a life entirely devoted to God, as will be that of the elect hereafter; a complete abandonment of the self into the hands of God, without expecting anything from man, or even from oneself; it is, literally a practice on this earth for the life hereafter. Thus, the religious life witnesses to men of the end which all human life ought to envisage, the end it has to reach if it is not to be a failure. In particular, it shows married persons the fulness of spiritual love which they should be approaching.

In the religious life, in the strict sense of the word, as in the Christian life generally, God 'makes no distinction between man and man' (Acts 10:34; Rom. 2:11); he pours forth his grace abundantly on all peoples. The Church's ancient monastic tradition, with its various historical developments, will impart to peoples lately introduced to Christianity an initial experience which is practically indispensable. But the Holy Spirit will, in addition, raise up new forms of the religious life, in harmony with the needs of the local Church and with individual vocations.

It must not be forgotten that each people has its special human characteristics, and, in consequence, its special way of adhering to Christ; for grace, when grafted on nature, perfects and sublimates its specific properties. The life of the Church in all its aspects vivifies all nations, but each of these has a vocation to exhibit, in a special way, one or another of them. Surely, the past history of India shows it as called to emphasize the mystical side of Christianity, and that of China to bring out its family spirit.

The clergy, whom the priesthood fits to discern different kinds of vocation, has to work for the 'rectification' of the special religious traditions of a people, that is, to bring out, over and above its too human tendencies or the errors intermingled with it, the spiritual aspirations set in their hearts by God, who, therefore, has given them a special aptitude to make manifest to the world. As Pope Pius XII declares, 'the Church has never disdained the doctrines held by pagans, but instead, after freeing them from all admixture of error, has completed and perfected them by the work of Christian wisdom' (*Evangelii Praecones*). In this way, the Church gives birth to new expressions of her ancient spirituality.

New Forms

The Church, being both one and Catholic, keeps unimpaired the unity which accrues from her union with Christ, and makes her capable of communicating the divine life to all peoples. She ever retains the universality which is bound up with her nature, which is hers by right from the beginning, by reason of her mystical identification with Christ. Yet her unity and catholicity both allow and demand differences which make up her adornment, and these arise from the differences between the peoples which it is her mission to take up 'as a body' into Christ. She unifies, without levelling, them, without stultifying their specific and original characters.

The catholicity of the Church demands of her the exhibition of her inexhaustible richness by expressing herself in all cultures, and by raising each of them to a really universal status through the elimination of what is exclusive. None of them will become identified with the Church, any more than the paste is identified with the yeast. Each will be a partial, limited expression. But all conjoined, each in its special way, have to lend their voices to the song the Church sings to the glory of the Creator, from whom all that is good comes to man.

Strictly speaking, the Church does not add to its intrinsic qualities when it takes different cultures to itself, when it incorporates the multitude of peoples, any more than the Son of God enriched himself in taking a human nature. What, then, do they bring to it? Their love for it, and for Christ? Certainly, this is a most precious thing, but, after all, it derives ultimately from the Church, which is alone able to communicate the Spirit. They may be said to bring their treasures of wisdom and knowledge, patience and endurance, beauty and heroism, accumulated through the centuries; and it is true that, under the dirt and blood sadly characteristic of human history, there gleam some grains of pure gold. These, however, are the work of God himself and of his Spirit which never ceases to guide men even when they stumble in the dark. All the goods of Christ belong of full right to the Church, his Spouse, which, in receiving the treasures of the various peoples, is but taking possession of what already belonged to it; and, in detaching them from their crudities, restores their true worth, benefits the whole of humanity, and offers each people unlimited possibilities of advancement.

Still, there is a sense in which each people brings something of its own to the Church. God himself, who is lacking in nothing and to whom all things belong, desires the love of men, and awaits their homage. In his Son 'it was God's good pleasure to let all completeness dwell, and through him to win back all things . . . into union with himself, making peace with them through his blood, shed on the cross' (Col. 1: 19-20). Yet, St Paul could say: 'In this mortal frame of mine, I help to pay off the debts which the afflictions of Christ leave still to be paid, for the sake of his body, the Church' (*Ibid*. 24).

What does this mean? All comes from God, and must return to him. No one can add to his fulness, but his gifts he makes over to his Church, to the peoples, for them to put to proper use, and restore to him as an act of freely given homage. The Church, born of God, is, as such, holy and perfect in itself. As God's gift to men, jointly with the Spirit, it is handed over to the peoples for them to make use of its riches on their own account, and to exhibit its inexhaustible wealth by the immense variety of goods they draw out from it. All the peoples are not too numerous for the work of showing forth in its full splendour the gift of God; it will never be perfectly achieved in the present life.

So it is that the Church makes all cultures fruitful, and enlightens them with the light of God. It thereby offers them the possibility of a hitherto unimagined development. Out of their treasures, always in a hidden way its own possession, it retains the best, the most typical, elements, to take them up in its own life, and give homage to God.

In so doing, the Church's life is, in a certain sense, modified, and it remains for us to examine the extent of this. The Christian life of the peoples is nourished from three sources, all deriving from the Church, but not all equally essential to it. *Divine Revelation* is absolutely primary, for, apart from it, there would be no supernatural life on earth. It is incapable of any modification, for it is strictly transcendent of all that is human. The sole question that arises in this connection is that of faithfully translating it into the various languages.

At the opposite extreme, what the Church uses as merely a *cultural expression* is, of its own nature, changeable, and capable of taking on many forms. The Church, in fact, expects, from its transplantation among new peoples, a luxuriant harvest. Feasts outside those of the liturgy, sacred art, spiritual and corporeal works, family observances, all take on a fresh and unusual colouring, and bring in unaccustomed harmonies to Christianity. Here a free rein is allowed to individual and social initiative, subject to the control of the hierarchy.

Between these two, *ecclesiastical tradition* acts as a mediator, for it binds closely together human elements and what comes from God. As entrusted with revelation, and handing it down in its totality, it defines doctrines in formularies where philosophy is called on as an auxiliary agent. It receives the sacraments from the hands of Christ, but directs their liturgical application by means of gestures and symbols borrowed from various sources. It preserves the Church's essential structure and the fundamental laws bequeathed by Christ, but has also to complete the formation of its different elements, and, in so doing, it is inspired by the administrative and legal systems worked out by the nations of the world. Though founded on the cornerstone which is Christ, and in so far unchangeable, tradition is, also, in part the work of the Church, which has received from its Head power to add subordinate parts to its structure to assist its functioning.

From this latter point of view, tradition is not rigidly uniform, and admits some degree of change. Almost from the very beginning, its unity was seen to be compatible with a plurality of forms, agreeing in the essential, but varying in outward character; these derive from manifold sources, Latin and Oriental, whose original nature the Church has striven to preserve all through her history. Very significant, too, is the way the liturgy has developed, both recurring to its sources in the past and adding certain new elements. A striking instance is the restoration by Pope Pius XII, first of the Paschal Vigil, then of the whole liturgy of Holy Week. The importance of the results intended makes it clear that it belongs to the hierarchy alone, while seeking the views of priests and the laity in general, to sort out the human resources at hand, and to decide at what moment, and how far, they ought to be incorporated in the living tradition.

The work to be done here cannot be hurried, and would only be delayed or hazarded by imprudent action. When the missionary casts on the earth the seed from which a local Church will spring, he may be able to introduce, there and then, a few changes of a quite superficial kind. A profounder development, however, needs to take place much more slowly, as it is the outcome of a vital assimilation. The different concrete possibilities must be carefully examined and their suitability estimated.

Of the various elements contributed, over the centuries, by Western civilization, to the Church, some have been applied universally, and made inseparable from those of divine origin; such are the allotment of distinct regions to individual members of the episcopal college, scholastic philosophy in its essential teachings, and the basic features of canon law. Other elements are an integral part of Christian life in the west, but are not applied elsewhere. Thus, the structure of the divine office is not the same in the Latin Church as in the Churches of the East; and there is reason to suppose that, in course of time, the Churches of Asia and Africa will have their own liturgy, in which their distinctive forms of prayer will be conjoined with the unchangeable form of the sacraments and the ancient Christian traditions. Yet other elements there are that seem better than any possible substitute, and specially suited to promote the spiritual life of all. Though not at all necessary for salvation, devotion to Our Lady of Lourdes, for example, or to Our Lady of Fatima, being neither typically French nor Portuguese, is naturally suited to persons all over the world. However 'western' may be a custom or an institution, it is not thereby unsuited for the Churches in other regions, and this applies still more to particular forms of the liturgy; the desire, in fact, to give such practices a native mode of expression must not degenerate into a narrow particularism. It is well to make use of what has been approved by long custom in other lands, and to recognize the superiority of certain elements of a western colouring; but this does not imply the rejection of new accretions, nor does it dispense from the need of receiving them gladly.

On the other hand, the assimilation of elements from Asiatic or African sources will not only bring into being forms of life suited to various peoples, but will throw light on valuable treasures practically ignored up to the present, though inherent in the nature of Catholicism, and destined to benefit all the Churches. The conditions for this, however, are not yet present. The missionary, however free from prejudice of any kind, and lovingly studious of the people he is sent to teach, yet, as a foreigner, can only with difficulty penetrate their inner nature, and very rarely becomes intimately acquainted with them. He can only prepare the way and form the local clergy who are capable of bringing the work to completion, inasmuch as they will have assimilated the living tradition of the Church, without losing their rootedness in the past of their own people.

The spontaneous reactions of the newly-converted deserve special attention, for they are not always precisely what the foreigner might expect. Their spiritual progress may, at times, baulk at certain customs that the missionary invites them to adopt, but, even more often, they reveal an aspiration to a thorough and complete change. The reason is that modes of conduct and action perfectly good and excellent in themselves easily appear to them as tainted with the religious errors with which they are historically connected. They are more keenly alive than ordinary Christians to the unique character of the Christian Revelation, and therefore desire to find an entirely new way of expressing it. In a newly constituted Church, especially, there is a strong desire to feel in communion with the universal Church, by using the same gestures, repeating the same prayers, and observing the same ceremonies. That is, undoubtedly, why one so often finds the natives of Chad and the Cameroons preferring the Latin chant to any other.

The missionary cannot remain merely passive in regard to this state of mind. 'All that in the customs of the peoples is not indissolubly bound up with religious error must always be studied in a friendly spirit, and, whenever possible, preserved and fostered' (Pius XII, *Summi Pontificatus*). Anything extreme in the nature of an 'iconoclastic' reaction against the past must be tempered. In any case, such a reaction is not permanent. From the days of the early Church, its members have taken up very different attitudes to the prevalent philosophy, forms of art, and customs. Some have been inclined to make a clean sweep of them; others, without underestimating the need for changing them, perceived the intrinsic value of these human acquisitions, and their aptitude to enrich the Christian life. The missionary to-day, while avoiding undue haste, and sedulously fostering the sense of Catholic unity both in the local clergy and in their flocks, will, at the same time, help them to perceive in their ancestral traditions gifts of God for the adornment of his Church.

Their philosophy may serve to introduce the minds of men to the Christian faith, to advance the traditional philosophy and make it an even better instrument of Revelation. The gestures of adoration and oblation inherited by the peoples from their forefathers, their traditional feasts and rites, may well have been, in certain respects, a rendering of true homage to God, and should be restored by incorporation with Christian worship. To sing the glory of God, all the languages and arts of men should contribute to the universal harmony. As the Church grows in stature, it needs to create the additional elements indispensable to its activities, and to reorganize those already in existence; it welcomes, for the purpose, any suggestions arising from native sources. Thus, it suffers none of God's gifts to man to perish, and continues to add to that variety of colour which makes the splendour of Catholic unity.

This does not imply any yielding to a temptation to archaeologize, nor does it involve an obstinate upholding of ways of thought and conduct already dying out. Neither philosophy, nor art, nor law, nor social customs, can be subjected to mere repetition, under pain of being thereby doomed to extinction. Life supposes movement, and, in consequence, continual development. The Church's adoption of elements of a culture is not just a matter of recognizing that this rule of law, or that type of art, is good in itself, and deciding to retain it. It is rather a matter of a fresh discovery, a new creation, inspired indeed by the experience both of the Christian and the national past.

A new cultural creation would be merely an artificial production, without life of its own, unless it were associated with the trend of the culture already in existence. At the present time, by reason of increased facilities of communication, and of the growing economic and political interdependence of all peoples, mankind is strongly impelled towards a world-wide culture. In consequence, abundant possibilities of advancement are offered to all peoples, but there is the danger of their becoming estranged to their own inheritance and of losing their specific personality. The flood which bears them on is irresistible, and makes useless any attempt merely to hold on to the past. The Church, however, is called to enter the stream in order to make it serve a Christian purpose. She is, in fact, providentially equipped with the means of canalizing it, and imprinting on it the seal of a catholicity which brings all things to a unity, without eliminating their varied richness. So it is that, as the 'fulness of Christ', she will have 'established all things' in him.

CONCLUSION

'THE Church's sole mission is that of bringing all men to share in the salvation brought by Christ's redemption, by spreading the kingdom of Christ over the entire world' (Pius XI, *Rerum Ecclesiae*). 'A disciple is no better than his master, a servant than his lord; enough that the disciple should fare like his master, the servant like his lord' (Mt. 10: 24-25). The Church's vocation is to walk in the footsteps of Christ; its whole mission, like his, is summed up as *Redemptive Incarnation*.

The Church *is incarnate* in the world, in the true sense; not an invention of man, but a creation of Christ; no mere assemblage of men, but the mystical body of Christ. Born of God, she makes God present among men. God is not changed thereby, but mankind is taken up, transformed, and made divine. The function of the Church is to take hold of human activity, whose source is God himself, to bring men to their final end, to make them participate in the life of the Trinity.

'See how all the gifts that make for life and holiness in us belong to his divine power; come to us through fuller knowledge of him, whose own glory and sovereignty have drawn us to himself! Through him God has bestowed on us high and treasured promises; you are to share the divine nature, with the world's corruption, the world's passions, left behind' (2 Pet. 1 : 3-4).

The Church, enlightener of men, shines out suddenly in the darkness, and her flame has a blinding quality. No man has the power to extinguish it, or to let its rays filter through at his own good pleasure. To attempt anything of the sort is to stand self-condemned. Thus, the Church, by her mere presence, acts as a judgment on mankind. She is made accessible to men through the medium of languages, which, without lessening her splendour or exhausting her mystery, refracts her in the manner of a prism, enabling men to look on her and divine something of her richness. Human signs, whether words or gestures, being of God's creation, are of themselves apt to signify what is divine, but, if they are to convey the transcendence of the divine word, they have to be taken over and transformed from within, under the guidance of the Spirit.

As the Word of God took hold of human nature to raise it to himself, so the Church empties herself in order to bring God the whole of mankind. As Christ, too, took on himself our human condition, so the Church subjects herself to human cultures to express herself in tangible form. She assumes them to purify and vitalize them, to bring to their highest potential the qualities, both natural and supernatural, with which God has endowed individuals and societies. In this way, she gathers mankind together in the unity of Christ, and makes it capable of receiving the life of the Trinity.

By becoming incarnate, the Church, like Christ, engages in warfare with the powers of evil which desire to keep the world under their sway. She will gain the victory only by *Redemption* in sacrifice. The success of her mission is not just a question of method. The most perfect love, the highest degree of knowledge, the most studied techniques, though they have their share in the ultimate result, are inadequate to guarantee the victory. The work of the mission cannot be estimated according to its visible results. Whatever be the wisdom, human and supernatural, that directs it, it must confront opposition and meet with setbacks; for victory comes from the Cross.

Like Christ, the Church is, and always will be, a scandal to men, for she refuses to serve their material interests or to compromise with their desires. The assured advance she brings to man is not of the temporal order. It involves a breach with the old, a dying, in order to live again on a higher plane of being.

The way of salvation passes by the Cross, which releases floods of living water on the world, and gives access to the *Resurrection*. At the side of Christ,—'his was the first birth out of death' (Col. 1 : 18)—the Church takes up her place, as his Spouse, and gathers within her the whole of mankind to reign with him in eternity.

'It was not you that chose me, it was I that chose you. The task I have appointed you is to go out and bear fruit, fruit which will endure' (Jn. 15: 16).

'A grain of wheat must fall into the ground and die,

or else it remains nothing more than a grain of wheat; but if it dies, then it yields rich fruit' (Jn. 12: 14).

'I saw in my vision that holy city which is the new Jerusalem, being sent down by God from heaven, all clothed in readiness, like a bride who has adorned herself to meet her husband. I heard, too, a voice which cried aloud from the throne, Here is God's tabernacle pitched among men; he will dwell with them, and they will be his own people, and he will be among them, their own God. He will wipe away every tear from their eyes, and there will be no more death, or mourning, or cries of distress, no more sorrow; these old things have passed away' (Apoc. 21: 2-4).

BIBLIOGRAPHY

Academia Studies, vols. 1 sq., 1943 sq., (New York, The America Press.)

AUPIAIS, *Le Missionnaire*. (Paris, Larose, 1938.)

BOULARD, F., *Introduction to Religious Sociology*. London, to be published by Darton, Longman & Todd, 1960. Tr. Fr. M. I. Jackson.

BRODERICK, J., *Saint Francis Xavier*. (London, Burns Oates, 1952.)

CAPERAN, L., *Le Problème du salut des infidèles*. (Toulouse, Grand Séminaire, 1934.)

CHARLES, P., *Les dossiers de l'action missionnaire*. (Louvain, Aucam, 1938.)

   Missiologie. (Louvain, Aucam, 1939.)

   Études missiologiques. (Paris, Desclée de Brouwer, 1956.)

China in the sixteenth century: the Journals of Matthew Ricci. Ed. by Gallagher. (New York, Randon House, 1953.)

CLARK, Fr. X., *The Purpose of Missions*. (New York, Missionary Union of the Clergy, 1948.)

CONGAR, Y., *Lay People in the Church*. (London, Bloomsbury, 1957.) Tr. D. Attwater.

CONSIDINE, J. M., *Across a World*. (London, Longmans, 1946.)

   Call for Forty Thousand. (London, Longmans, 1946.)

COSTANTINI, Mgr., *L'art chrétien dans les missions*. (Paris, Desclée de Brouwer, 1949.)

CRONIN, V., *The Wise Man from the West*. (London, Hart Davis, 1955.)

   The Pearl of India. (London, Hart Davis, 1959.)

DANIÉLOU, J., *God and Us*. (London, Mowbray, 1957.) Tr. Fr. W. Roberts.

   Advent. (London, Sheed and Ward, 1950.) Tr. Rosemary Sheed.

   The Lord of History. (London, Longmans, 1958.) Tr. Nigel J. Abercrombie.

Holy Pagans of the Old Testament. (London, Longmans, 1957.) Tr. Fr. F. Faber.

FENTON, J. C., *Catholic Church and Salvation.* (Westminster, Maryland, Newmans.)

KOROLEVSKY, C., *Living Languages in Catholic Worship.* (London, Longmans, 1957.) Tr. D. Attwater.

Lima Methode Conference. (Maryknoll Publications, Maryknoll (New York).)

LOFFELD, E., *Le problème cardinal de la missiologie et des missions catholiques.* (Rhenen, Hollande, 1957.)

LUBAC, H. de, *Catholicism.* (London, Burns Oates & Washbourne, 1950.) Tr. L. C. Sheppard.

    Le fondement théologique des missions. (Paris, Le Seuil, 1946.)

MENASCE, J. de, 'Polarité de l'activité missionnaire', *Nouvelle Revue de Science Missionnaire*, 1945.

Mission Specialists' Conferences Proceedings, (5 vol.). (New York, Fordam University Press, 1953.)

MONTCHEUIL, (Y. de), *Aspects de l'Eglise.* (Paris, Cerf, 1951.)

MURPHY, E. L., *Teach Ye all Nations.* (Benziger, New York, 1958.)

OLIVER, R., *The Missionary Factor in East Africa.* (London, Longmans, 1952.)

The Popes on the Missions. (London, Sword of the Spirit, 1958.)

Des prêtres noirs s'interrogent. (Paris, Cerf, 1956.)

RETIF, A., *Foi au Christ et Mission.* (Paris, Cerf, 1953.)

SEUMOIS, A., *Introduction à la missiologie.* (Ed. Nouvelle Revue Science Missionnaire, 1952.)

SUENENS, Mgr., *The Gospel to Every Creature.* (London, Burns Oates & Washbourne, 1958.)

VOILLAUME, R., *Seeds of the Desert.* (London, Burns Oates & Washbourne, 1955.) Tr. Fr. W. Hill.

WU, J. C. H., *Beyond East and West.* (London, Sheed & Ward, 1952.)

INDEX

145